SPIRITUAL DIRECTION:
AN INVITATION TO
ABUNDANT LIFE

D0498892

SPIRITUAL DIRECTION: AN INVITATION TO ABUNDANT LIFE

by
Francis W. Vanderwall, S.J.

with a Foreword by
Henri J. M. Nouwen

PAULIST PRESS
New York/Ramsey

Library of Congress
Catalog Card Number: 81-83185

ISBN: 0-8091-2399-1

Published by Paulist Press
545 Island Road, Ramsey, N.J. 07446

Printed and bound in the
United States of America

CONTENTS

FOREWORD ix

AUTHOR'S PREFACE 1

Prologue
THE INVITATION 3

Chapter One
WHO NEEDS SPIRITUAL DIRECTION? 7

Chapter Two
WHAT HAPPENS THROUGH SPIRITUAL DIRECTION? . 11

Chapter Three
WHAT TO LOOK FOR IN A SPIRITUAL DIRECTOR 49

ACKNOWLEDGMENTS

Many people have given of their knowledge and of themselves in the evolution of this book. I am deeply grateful to each one of them and regret that their numbers preclude the listing of their names here. However, I would like to thank the Yale Divinity School and particularly Henri J. M. Nouwen for giving me the space and encouragement needed to embark on this work. I also thank those who through their criticisms, suggestions and friendship enabled me to continuously keep drawing out of myself resources that I never knew existed.

I thank particularly John Veltri, S.J., Ernest Larkin, O. Carm., Leo Rock, S. J., Rev. Carey Landry, Don Gelpi, S. J., Sr. Marian Cowan, C.S.J., David Fleming, S.J., Chaplain David Duncombe, and Jim LaCasse, S.J. Special thanks also go to my friends at Moye Formation Centre, especially Sr. Dianne Heinrich, C.D.P., Sr. Nicole Bunnell, C.D.P., and Sr. Anne Michele Berry, C.D.P., without whose love and support many of these pages may never have materialized. I am indebted to Mrs. Velma Baumann as well, who helped me put this manuscript into correct English, and to those who typed it for me. To them I am very grateful.

To my mother and father
who first introduced me to the life of the Spirit,
and to each of you
who have nurtured me along the way since,
with love and gratitude

FOREWORD

When Francis Vanderwall came to Yale Divinity School to interrupt his busy life as a spiritual director and to recreate his mind and spirit, he soon discovered the best way to use this unique opportunity. Unlike many others at the university, it seemed that his task was not to acquire new knowledge, meet new people, and experience new situations, but to take ample time to reflect on and write about the unusually rich years during which he had been a spiritual guide. This book is the tangible result. I am very grateful that Francis let me be part of the early stages of his writing and that he asked me to introduce the final text to the readers.

I have seldom read a book on the spiritual life and spiritual direction that is so grounded—so "gutsy"—as this. On every page I can feel that Francis speaks from experience—not just from a rich experience of living, but also from a profound experience of the presence of God in the midst of all the living. By writing this book, Francis Vanderwall has made a significant contribution to the understanding of what it means to live a spiritual life in our contemporary society and what it means to ask for and offer guidance in the life of the Spirit. There are three elements of this book which make it such a significant contribution.

First of all Francis shows clearly and convincingly that the spiritual life and spiritual direction is not something for special Christians. His many true-to-life stories make it clear that every human being is called, and able, to live a life guided by the Spirit. In these pages we encounter not a group of pious churchgoers, but people deeply involved in the human struggle for physical, mental and emotional survival. We meet a harried college dean, a confused seminarian, a reluctant undercover policeman, a guilt-ridden murderer, a violent truck driver and many other real people. These very different personalities all share the desire for some direction in finding God's presence in the midst of their turmoil.

Secondly, Francis has the courage not to hide his own weaknesses. Thus he lets his readers sense that spiritual direction is quite different from a distant advice-giving. While deeply formed by the Ignatian tradition of spiritual direction and well trained in the underlying theological disciplines, Francis never presents himself as a "professional." In this book he shows that spiritual direction is a ministry of sweat and tears, not without agony and even moments of despair. Better than anyone I know, Francis stresses that spiritual direction always leads to a fellowship of the weak. This makes this book a truly compassionate book that is as valuable for those who give spiritual guidance as it is for those who receive it.

Finally Francis restates in many ways and on many pages the central mystery of the spiritual life: the director, guide, counselor, comforter and healer is not the well-trained human person, but God himself. Spiritual direction does not mean that one spiritual person tells another less spiritual person what to think, say or do in order to become a more spiritual person. It is not the knower speaking to the ignorant. Spiritual direction means that two or more sinful, broken, struggling people come together to listen to the direction of the Spirit. Francis stressed over and over that it is not *he* but the Spirit of God who guides, directs, heals, comforts and opens new perspectives; that it is not *he* who offers love, joy, peace and gentleness, but that it is the Spirit of God who offers these gifts in abundance. It is this mystery of God's guidance and God's gifts that make this such a freeing and playful book. Francis becomes in his own book a fool for Christ who offers little else than his own weak humanity and thus opens the way for his tense, nervous, agonizing and often deeply distressed fellow travelers to recognize with heart and mind that God's love is greater than any human pain. Thus no reader can escape the realization that the spiritual director is as dependent on God's grace as the one he or she directs, and no reader can avoid the challenge that prayer is the beginning and end of all spiritual assistance.

While reading and rereading this book I felt truly encouraged—not because I became convinced that I was better than I thought, nor because I was reassured that I did better than I feared, but because I came to a renewed awareness that my own sins, failings and struggles were infinitely small when seen in the light of God's abundant love and that my very real limitations in helping others could in fact become the gateways through which God makes this abundant love known to others. Thus this book helped me to smile and not judge, helped me to feel loved and not condemned, and helped me to be confident in God's presence in all that I am doing and not doubting all the time the value of my life and work.

I am very glad Francis wrote this book. The awareness that many will read it and feel freer because of it is a true source of joy for me. In the midst of our violent, harsh and often merciless world this gentle, compassionate, non-judgmental and caring book is a true treasure.

—Henri J. M. Nouwen

AUTHOR'S PREFACE

There is always the fear in a book of this sort of being misunderstood. I feel it necessary to say a few words at the very beginning that will hopefully dispel some of that concern.

This work is the result of several years of personal experiences in the life of the Spirit. I have been awed and many times deeply moved by the various signs of the Holy Spirit in my life and in the lives of others. What I have tried to do here is share some of these experiences with you. And here is where my initial difficulties began. I soon realized that I was going to have to make myself vulnerable, reveal my various needs and run the danger of exposing my inner struggles and weaknesses as I tried to describe the world of the spirits to you. After much prayer and after many discussions with friends I decided to take that risk, feeling that the value of sharing the world of the spirits with others outweighed the fear within me.

My next difficulty evolved out of the realization that in order to describe the world of the spirits as is, I needed to include many examples of the movements of the spirits in people, and I had to be truthful in this. Yet, I had to also handle with extreme care the knowledge entrusted to me by others. Again after many deliberations and discussions with friends and experts I decided to keep all the movements of the spirits intact and drastically alter all external and identifiable circumstances. Matters started looking much better but I was still not content. So finally, whenever I felt that there might be the slightest possibility of confidentiality being violated, I contacted the person concerned and secured permission from that person to use his or her story in this book. Hence the examples I have used will hopefully represent accurately some of the movements of the spirits and nothing of the people involved in them.

Finally, I had a problem with language. Given the very healthy contemporary movement toward non-exclusivity in the use of the personal pronoun, I have tried to eliminate all forms of "he" and "she" and used "one" instead. If I have slipped here and there, it is only because the language could not contain it and not for any other reason.

It is hoped that in these pages you will find the encouragement to go on if you have already entered the happy world of your deeper, Spirit-guided self, and if you are yet deliberating as to its value, I trust that the freedoms and joys I have here tried to describe give you the needed incentive to allow that beauty within you to flower forth.

Prologue
THE INVITATION

This writing is evolving out of my own experiences in the life of the Spirit, both within myself and in others. It is hence an intensely personal accounting, but also one that has direct parallels in others. The reflections I offer you then are not so much intended as directives or points for study, though some of them may stimulate discussions that could well lead to that, but rather offer concrete manifestations of the glory of God in the day-to-day of our lives. In a world steeped in values that are non-spiritual, this work offers a counter-point. And it is not alone in this offer, for all around us there are signs of a strong revival of longing occurring in the hearts of men and women for matters spiritual. The contemporary charismatic movements, the recent initiatives for peace and justice, and the resurgence of interest, especially among the young, for encounter groups and the like are well known and provide tangible signs of this revival. It is one that was perhaps triggered by the fresh breezes of Vatican Council II, or by strong feelings of dissatisfaction with the superficiality of our lives, but whatever the point of origin the Spirit is freshly moving among his people, and we are being challenged to listen once again to his voice. In the clattering of a contemporary world milieu this is not always an easy task, and it calls for an alertness in one's heart, a willingness in one's mind, and an openness to a "gentle breeze" for his sound to become audible.

Here I offer you a support for this. By hearing of his movements already occurring, you may perhaps begin to recognize those same movements within yourself. By learning of his ways and the triumphs he works in his people you may derive a hope for perseverance, and by knowing of the struggles inherent in responding to the Spirit you may be encouraged to work through your own struggles and so arrive at a freedom of mind and heart that we all so long for.

Out of this hope the format of this work has evolved. It is intended to serve both those seeking direction in their spiritual lives as well as those directing others, for in the spiritual life we soon realize that we need many supports to encourage us along our pilgrim way. This becomes evident even as we begin our journey, for the subtleties and ambiguities inherent in the spirit world are many and we need help discerning the various movements going on within us. This is because the Holy Spirit who longs to heap blessings and all good things upon us has an active adversary in the evil spirit who unceasingly works to prevent this from happening. The resulting battle that has raged from time immemorial in the minds and hearts of people everywhere is evidenced in the struggles we all experience in choosing between good and evil in our lives.

In order to aid the eventual triumphing of the good within us we seek help from various people and numerous sources so that we can with a greater facility cooperate with the graces of the Holy Spirit so readily available to all who believe. This work is offered as an aid in this process, even as spiritual directors offer help to those seeking God's will in their lives.

And this is the crux of the matter. It is what spiritual direction is all about. To be able to cooperate with the voice of the Spirit within us and, by obediently listening to that voice, permit the realization of God's will to take place within our lives. And his will is always directed toward our greater good, never lesser. His will is for life, and for life more abundantly.

But how do we go about cooperating with the Spirit within us? As much as we may want to do it, the world of the Spirit is by and large a world of mystery, operating very much out of a quite different set of realities than we are accustomed to in this world. Cooperating with the Spirit becomes a tricky maneuver and often we are tempted to give up on it because of its unfamiliar and tenuous nature in our daily lives. Compared to earning a living, trying our best to make ends meet each month, paying the bills that have to be paid, and answering the telephone, it is not at all surprising that the subtleties of the spiritual life appear to pass us by.

But do they? The world of the Spirit is as much a part of our daily world as our morning cup of coffee may be. It participates in our world of feelings, inner inclinations, hopes, visions and dreams. It is the very stuff that our daily routines are made of, for in the Spirit's cajolings, urgings and scoldings many a daily action receives its motivation. The world of the spirits is comprised of both good and bad movements. We learn to recognize them and differentiate the one from the other by looking for the symptoms within us. So, when we find, for example, a feeling of anger or sadness in prayer unaccompanied by any previous cause we have a possible symptom of something evil seeking to make us unhappy. On the other hand a feeling of genuine delight, in a passage from Scripture, for example, that leaves us with a lasting peace, may very well be a symptom of the good spirit, the Spirit of God. I say "may be a symptom," for sometimes the discerning of that spirit a little further could indicate quite another source—an evil spirit disguised as a good one. It is precisely because of such subtleties that we need help in our spiritual lives. Fortunately for us, many a spiritual writer has already provided us with the necessary rules and regulations we need for the enterprise. One of the finest of these is the Rules for the Discernment of Spirits in *The Spiritual Exercises of St. Ignatius Loyola*. Many translations and several interpretations of this classic writing enable easy access today to this work.

Listening to the voice of the spirits within us can be an exciting adventure in which we get in contact with all that is most lasting and most true about ourselves. We need to believe that when we begin listening to ourselves, to the various movements going on in our feelings in prayer, we are in fact listening to the Holy Spirit as well as to the spirits of darkness. I must emphasize that the feelings and movements I am talking about are primarily connected to those experienced while in prayer, though certainly the feelings we experience when we witness a terrible accident, let us say, are not to be excluded. For the spirit world is all encompassing and is certainly not a compartmentalized world restricted to our periods of prayer alone. It permeates all that we do and hence deserves the particular attention of periods devoted entirely to its nurturing. However, I am emphasizing the movements that occur while in prayer because we begin to enter the world of spirits through this door, and it is out of prayer that we gradually come to see the links between this world, redeemed and loved as it is, and the Spirit world and all that it offers us of love, of hope and of faith.

All of us are invited to live in the Spirit, and we need help to do this. But does this mean that all of us need spiritual direction? I begin my work by trying to answer that question in a realistic way. Then I deal with the consequences of entering into the world of the spirits and allowing the richness of the Holy Spirit to touch our lives. Finally I try to outline some of the qualifications one can legitimately expect from a spiritual director.

It is an exciting world we have been invited into. In it we are like adventurers exploring uncharted territories. We have been invited, and so we feel confident in our own abilities, yet we are always alert for signs of trouble ahead. As we journey onward toward the glory that is already ours, it is heartening to pause awhile and be reaffirmed in the faith we have in our expedition, in our Leader, and in ourselves by recognizing the signs around us that that glory is already in our midst.

Those who choose to allow the Lord to work in their lives cannot remain unchanged, and while the change may not always be a dramatic conversion experience it is nevertheless one that profoundly changes the very core of one's being. After encountering a living Father-Son-Spirit one cannot again be the same. It is to celebrate this truth that I write, and I pray that all those who share these pages with me may derive from them hope for perseverance as we continue on our pilgrim way to him who loves us so dearly.

Chapter One
WHO NEEDS
SPIRITUAL DIRECTION?

The life of the spirit is all inclusive and demands that we acknowledge its pervading influence in our lives. For even as the life of the body calls for an attentiveness to be properly nurtured so also does the life of the spirit. Accordingly, even as we need to eat, to get rest, and take care of our health, we also need to devote a certain care to our spirit if we want it to develop and mature. We cannot neglect it and expect it to take care of itself; it too needs physicians and demands that one follow their recommendations.

Does this mean that all people need spiritual directors at some time or another in their lives? If the above analogy is to hold water it appears that the answer lies in the affirmative. But this just does not fit the reality of the situation, for, in fact, the vast majority have not received spiritual direction, and many simple Christians working in the obscurity of a farming community, let us say, certainly do not receive spiritual direction. Yet they may possess a sanctity that many who have received it for years do not have. Are we to say then that in some way or another they are spiritually impoverished, or, worse still, belong to a lower "class" of spirituality? Or, is the reverse of that the case? Are there some specially chosen, "a privileged class" if you will, who receive routinely the special benefits of spiritual direction and hence have an inside track on holiness?

The very thought is abominable. Of course not! Of course

there are no classes of people in the spiritual world. Of course all are equal in the eyes of God, far more in fact than in this world of sin. And of course there does not exist any discrimination in the spiritual life, an unfair division between the haves and the have nots! Holiness is available to all people, "to Jews as well as Greeks," to believers in Jesus as well as to others who have never heard of him. Holiness is available to the world, to every person in his or her own particular circumstances. God gives to all equally the necessary means to salvation and offers his gifts as we need them to attain this end. The Lord did come to save all people, even those who have not yet even heard of his name!

So, what do we do with the contention that all people appear to need spiritual direction? It seems to me that the question is handled by first clarifying what is meant by spiritual direction. I feel that many, especially those engaged in directing others spiritually, may develop an understanding of the phrase that is inaccurate. When we speak of it we think of a person dispensing suggestions and guidelines that will help another improve spiritually and get closer to God. But there are surely many other ways of getting closer to God besides having a conversation with another person. There is, for example, the person who has a spiritual insight about something, who then discusses it with a close friend, a spouse maybe, and receives some clarifications on it from that person. Or perhaps there is the person who in reading a book, any book, receives an insight that enables that person to understand better some interior movement or feeling that was troubling. And then there is the very excellent way of getting spiritual direction through the sacrament of reconciliation. This has been rendered far easier now with the new rite that enables a spiritual conversation to take place as a part of the reconciliation with God offered in the sacrament. And then there is the public way of getting direction through the Sunday homily that for most Christians, at any rate, is the only source of spiritual guidance. And who does not know of the person who after the homily has sought out the homilist for a clarification or further explanation of some point or other in the homily? In this spiritual direction is taking place.

Spiritual direction comes in many forms and is hence not restricted to a one-to-one conversation, though it is certainly an extraordinarily helpful tool when you can get it. The fact is that many have become very holy without it and may well continue to do so. The Holy Spirit is not restricted and is quite capable of leading his people without a qualified human instrument to help him. Often an incompetent director—I would describe one of those as a person who feels he is competent only because of training and not because of the Holy Spirit—has done a sincere person much harm. Many a time I have talked with people who left prayer alone, in fact even abandoned the sacraments, because of one such encounter with a spiritual director who was incompetent. In a case like this it is evident that the person would have been far better off without a spiritual director than with one.

The point is that not everyone needs a particular person who regularly provides spiritual guidance. Everyone does need spiritual direction, however, in that all of us need clarifications, interpretations, and suggestions for improvement in our inner lives. At certain times in one's life one feels the need to talk on an on-going basis with a particular person about spiritual matters, and at that time one may seek out someone for this guidance, but it is not something that is going to occur throughout one's life. On the other hand spiritual direction is not to be considered something reserved for crisis times alone. I don't mean that direction is like a suicide hot-line. Far from it. I rather see it as helpful when one is taking another step forward in the life of the Spirit. And the time between steps, the time of growth and maturation in that particular step, may be accomplished with the help of the Holy Spirit in his many manifestations. If one has a spiritual director as well, all well and good, but the lack of one does not indicate an inability to grow in the life of the Spirit.

I suppose that seeing a director could be compared to the regular checkups advised by the medical profession for the proper care of our bodies. They obviously don't mean that we should see a doctor every time we get the sniffles, but rather ask that we do get the checkups so that the times between them may be healthy, or at least may be times of minimal ill health. Accordingly we can see a director for guidance, and go to him as a spiritual physician when we feel we are spiritually not very strong, but after receiving the director's help we could reasonably be expected to handle the times of the spiritual sniffles on our own. So we all need a spiritual director at various times in our lives but we certainly are not helpless to respond to God's graces without one. If we have easy access to one, by all means the gift is to be used, but when we don't we must not be afraid of floundering. God's grace is always near and will reach us through some other means.

Further, as should be evident by now, spiritual direction is not the domain of religious and priests alone. It belongs to all people intent on developing their interior lives. Hence it stands to reason that spiritual directors are not restricted to priests and religious. It calls for a different set of qualifications—overlapping at many points, it is true, but nevertheless not to be identified with the requirements for religious vows or priestly ordination.

The spirit world, just like the world of medicine, needs competent guides to help people become whole, holier persons. But it always has such a Guide, in the dynamic presence of the Holy Spirit. He is available to all people, at all times, and is not restricted to any particular form of communication with his people. He is the Divine Healer who eagerly reaches out to help no matter the hour. Everyone needs him and in him all people receive guidance if they but want it.

Chapter Two
WHAT HAPPENS THROUGH SPIRITUAL DIRECTION?

A. Beyond the "How To" Books

All of us want to pray, and accordingly we seek out the various books that tell us how to do it. We receive help in their implementation from spiritual directors, and wonder as to our progress.

In this chapter I offer you some consequences of prayer in people's lives, and in their progress I pray that you find encouragement. I have read numerous books and articles that have told me how to pray but I feel that we also need to hear what happens after the "how to" books have been mastered. I am indebted to the "how to" books; they have helped many people, and many have been changed because of them, but there is a longing in our hearts, especially those of us who have struggled with prayer for years, to know what happens once the fruits of prayer have ripened and the "how to" books have been implemented.

The great mystics have told us of the transports of joy and rapture that have overwhelmed them, but who among us feels an affinity with them in our mostly ordinary spiritual lives? We may long for what a Teresa of Avila or a John of the Cross visioned, but we do not have a natural affinity with them. Yet the spiritual life is for all, not just for the uniquely blessed, and hence I offer some experiences that are of ordinary folk, people who struggle with the million-and-one distractions that the contemporary world offers, who work regular hours, and pay annual taxes, people who long for solitude but can only find it when driving to work, people who believe in a loving God but are compelled to find him in washing dishes and dusting furniture—people who dare to dream, though, of being great pray-ers, of being in union with a God in whom all their hopes, longings and fantasies may one day be fulfilled.

All of us are called to be saints, to be holy as our heavenly Father is holy. All of us have it within ourselves to be far holier than we are. Prayer is the exciting adventure of realizing this in companionship with God. It is a process that takes a lifetime, and then some, to be fully realized. This is why we seek spiritual direction—because deep down inside us, unspoken perhaps but nevertheless experienced, we know that there is more, much more, than the superficiality of the daily grind, and we long for the depths of our beings to be evoked so that the deep within us may be united to the deep of God, as the psalmist so well said it, and so become people of a potential fully realized but not yet. In this process, embarked on in faith, we quickly recognize that abstract notions become soon compressed and eventually set aside. The abstractions become submerged and take a very secondary place to an essentially dynamic relationship that is quite human, fearfully intimate, and wonderfully Jesus, both our God and our lover.

Maturing prayer moves from abstractions to a person. And in the encounter with this person, Jesus, we meet love, and as any lover knows there begin the real fireworks: the struggles, disappointments, joys, and glories that indeed make a life of prayer the most fulfilling experience of our lives. In it the glory of God becomes concretized, and we look for that future glory no longer with a cold and abstract faith but, having met it in love, with eager expectancy that draws us out of ourselves in a way that only a human God can do. Prayer is a love affair with an all too human God, and the more we surrender to prayer the more we are surrendering to him, in love and in faith. It is an affair that encompasses all of life then, even as love engulfs all of life, for prayer is not so much doing something as it is a living out of a love affair with a God who is personally involved with our hearts.

B. What the Spirit Brings

The gifts or fruits of the Holy Spirit are the visible signs of the

Spirit working in us. When we acquiesce to our love affair with God we are acquiescing to these gifts from him. They represent all that we long for—the hopes of our youth, the dreams of our aged, the visions of the forlorn. They speak of love and peace, of gentleness and the good we all so desire; they speak of a belonging in kinship to the whole world; they speak of patience and a lasting joy that is available for all of us who trust in the central vision of God's love.

The gifts invite us to share in the greatness of God, to become his sons and daughters, rich in his heritage of eternal and abiding love. They invite us to conversion, away from the small world of selfishness and sin to a world of greatness, bursting with hope and freedom where "there will be no more death, and no more mourning or sadness" (Rev. 21:4).

But gifts, in order to be given, presume that there is someone to give them to. One of the serious impediments that one finds among nominal Christians is a sense of futility and a refusal to accept themselves as sinners. It appears that unless we allow hope to be present when facing the reality of our sinfulness, it is hard for the Spirit to give himself to us. We must first accept ourselves as forgiven sinners and so enable the Spirit's gifts to be given to us.

When we feel unworthy of God's forgiving love we are allowing pride entrance, for in essence what is being said is: "I am such a great sinner, even God's love is not enough, so why even try?" This is dangerous talk and could lead to an unhealthy sense of dejection and eventual shutting out of any possibility of grace. Of course we are sinners, of course we fail, but the whole point of the story of redemption is that God loved us so much that he sent his only Son to free us from ourselves and gift us with his own love. The gifts of the Holy Spirit are given as manifestations of this one gift, God himself. It is up to us to recognize that God has accepted us for who we are and loved us nevertheless, as his own sons and daughters. He wants to show us signs of this acceptance through gifting us with himself in his many manifestations.

There is only one Gift. I think it important to stress that the various gifts of the Spirit are really various sides of the richness of God. They could be compared to a sparkling diamond that is slowly rotated in front of a light. As God gives us the gift of patience, let us say, it would be like a particular cut of the diamond sparkling brightly, but even as that cut sparkles, the beauty of the diamond as a whole is enhanced. So, patience would evoke peace and love, and so on.

The gifts are offered to all people but not to all indiscriminately. God gives us now one gift, then another, even as the particular need arises for that specific gift. So, it is good to be aware of what one's particular need is at any given moment in time. If today I feel quite impatient, let us say, I would need to pray in a particular way for the gift of patience, knowing that patience when received would enhance my general well-being. Hence I could also become more loving, more peace-filled, and receive an enhancement of all the gifts of the Spirit in the process. The gifts are distinct even as they are all facets of the one gift that is God.

Let us now go deeper into the world of the Spirit in his many manifestations and witness in them glimpses of the abundant life we all so long for. I trust that through these accounts of the Spirit already alive in his people, all those receiving spiritual direction will be given hope and confirmation of their own immense worth before God. And for those given to direct others in their spiritual lives, I pray that these examples confirm their conviction of the importance of their task as enablers of the life of the Spirit in this world that God loves so much.

"The Spirit and the Bride say, 'Come.' Let everyone who listens answer, 'Come.' Then let all who are thirsty come: all who want it may have the water of life, and have it free" (Rev. 22:17).

Love

The most visible sign in a person who is praying is a change of attitude, a change of heart if you will. "I shall pour clean water over you and you will be cleansed. . . . I shall give you a new heart, and put a new spirit in you" (Ez. 36:25). One who gives himself over to the process of love is surrendering to a conversion. One will never be the same again, and the changes that begin to take place in one's life, imperceptible though some of them may be, will lead to a greater peace, a deeper trust and a perduring happiness that even the stormiest of storms cannot shipwreck. The gift of love begins in the gift of admitting one's own lovableness. It is out of that conviction that we can go forth confidently to love others.

Once a person came to me seeking to learn the rudiments of meditation. He told me that he had been saying his prayers for years, went to Mass regularly, received the sacraments frequently, and still felt that "nothing was happening." He had mentioned this to a friend of his who suggested that he make a retreat. And here he was, seeking and longing for something more out of his prayer than he was receiving.

I listened to him and then asked him whether he had ever tried meditation on Scripture. He replied in the negative. I suggested that he try it and gave him some simple techniques as to procedure. I told him to find some quiet time in his day, set it aside for meditation and begin a daily routine of listening attentively to various Scripture passages in his heart. I pointed out the importance of listening to one's feelings while pondering Scripture, for it is there that God speaks with a great eloquence. I then gave him various Scripture passages to meditate on, each one dealing with some aspect of God's love for his people. "Stick to it," I advised, "and your life will begin to change." As I spoke he was writing my words down assiduously, and when I had finished he looked up, asked certain questions for clarification, and left. There was a hope in his face and an eagerness about his eyes as he set forth on his journey. He started meditating, and adhered, with a great fidelity, to the instructions I had given him. Gradually, over a period of months, things started changing for him. He walked in one day and told me about it. "I don't really believe it," he said, "but when you first told me that my life would change if I started these meditations I didn't believe you. I told myself: Let's wait and see." He had serious problems with his wife, two of his teenage sons were on drugs, there was financial stress in his business, and his in-laws kept telling him how to run his life. "Well, the problems I told you about are still there," he went on, "but the neat thing about them is that they are not bugging me anymore. I can handle them in ways I never could before." I asked him why he made the connection between his meditations and the changed attitude he now had. "Because I now know I am loved," he replied, "for who *I am,* a special unique person. There is no one else in the whole world like me." He smiled and added, "You know, the problems are going away too. I can feel it. I don't mean they are ending, but now I see that they fit, that God is asking me to carry them for him, so that I can become more like him in suffering.'' He began seeing his difficulties in a new light; his trials became redemptive because he saw, in prayer, that God had given them meaning. The thing that touched me was the way his meditation led him into a conversion of heart, where in the encounter with a loving God he learned not only to accept life's struggles, but to embrace them as meaning-filled gifts from his God. He saw that his difficulties were signs of God's love for him. Here is an instance, not dramatic, not powerful, but truly a story of conversion. And it happened when a man started praying.

To love oneself has been a Christian taboo for so long that speaking of it often causes embarrassment. Yet if we do not take that as a starting point, how can we love someone else? If I feel that I am unlovable and have nothing of worth to give, how can I genuinely offer love to someone else? I once remember meeting a most lovable old lady who was filled with doubts as to her own worth. For years she had tried to offer people tokens of her love and affection, usually through gifts of her own making. She crocheted and turned out exquisitely beautiful needlework designs. But even while she gave those tokens of her affection away, she felt that they were futile, unappreciated and forgotten. She "knew" the people who received them did so only out of courtesy to her and did not really care for them at all, let alone care for the person who made them. Throughout her life she had been brought up to believe that any admission of self-worth was bordering on pride and was sinful. In some way God would be angry with her if she admitted her talents to herself. Consequently, when people thanked her and expressed their gratitude to her for her gifts she could not hear them, feeling only that they were merely being conventional and didn't really mean any of it in their hearts.

Yet she wasn't a difficult lady. When we talked about her spiritual life she became enthusiastic and more than cooperative in telling me all about her prayers. She loved to pray and found much consolation in "talking to God." "Do you believe he loves you?" I asked, taking her gnarled, beautiful hands into mine. Her eyes took on a sparkle as she said, "Oh, yes, I know he does. But that's because he is God, not because I am any good." "What do you mean?" I asked, noticing that the sparkle in her eyes had diminished as quickly as it had arisen. "Well, I am a sinful person, and I've been full of all kinds of fears and anxieties throughout my life that one day I will be punished. Because of this I've become quite scrupulous over the years, and I guess I try to pacify God by being extra nice to people." She gave me a wry smile, as if to say, "But I don't really believe it helps!" "But we all sin," I said. "That's the whole point of Jesus' coming to save us, so that we can be forgiven. I know you believe that." "Oh sure," she replied, "but it's hard at times really feeling it's O.K., that my sins are really all forgiven, because I'm not sure whether I'm really sorry for them, in confession." "But you want to be, don't you?" I said, wanting very much to give her a warm embrace. "Oh, sure," she replied. "O.K., then, let God take it from there. Trust him to have forgiven you." "I suppose so," she said, and smiled wryly again.

I was still holding her hands. Allowing some moments to pass in silence, I looked straight at her eyes. She was really a lovable old lady, full of a gentleness that her age had matured over the years. There was a hope in her eyes as she looked back at me, but also an underlying sense of futility. "Mary," I said, "you are a lovable person, and I assure you I find you very special." With that I arose, lifting her up with me, and gave her a warm embrace.

She started to cry. "Do you really think so?" she mumbled between her tears. "Yes," I said, "I really do, and I see in you an awful lot of the love of God." She cried for a while, then stopped briefly to wipe her tears away. "Do you think God has forgiven me all my sins?" she asked. "Of course," I said. "He thinks you're kind of special, you know." She smiled wanly, then looked up, that sparkle in her eyes again. "You know, I think you are right." She paused, then sat down. "I'm feeling better," she said. "I'm feeling like I'm beginning to believe that he loves me special." "Good," I said. "That is the truth, you know. You are loved. How do you suppose you have had all that love to give all these years if he wasn't loving you first?" She looked up. "You know, I've never thought of it like that," she said and smiled. "I guess I must be kind of special to him." "Oh, yes," I said, "you are. Believe that!"

That conversation, a simple exchange, marked a significant and lasting change in her life. It was the starting point of a process of self-awareness that brought her a kind of confidence that she didn't have before. The gift of the Spirit taught her of his love in a way she had not been aware of, and this in turn generated a whole new attitude within her. Now when people thank her for her gifts, she accepts their thanks and actually delights in their praise. Now she enjoys making the gifts much more, for she feels that they are not bribes but genuine signs of her love.

The gift of love is a gift of the Spirit. And this he instills in us in so many ways, even through a simple conversation. It is difficult, at times, admitting the Spirit's work, so caught up are we in expecting his signs to be dramatic and of great consequence, but he is most certainly at work whenever one person begins to appreciate herself a little more and starts believing that she has love to give. From here the power of love begins, and when unleashed can be a force so powerful that the whole world cannot contain it.

A former student of mine once remarked that for all the talking that goes on about love, he found very little loving going on at the college he was attending. He would attend the Saturday evening liturgies, talk to fellow students there, and even attend the occasional socials the Christian Students' Union would stage once in a while. But there was a point beyond which Christianity did not go, and the longer he found himself at the school the more disillusioned he became with ever establishing a lasting friendship with any of the students there. The matter was not helped by the fact that he was quite shy and felt awkward in social settings. He did not know how to reach out, as much as he longed to do, and no one in the group apparently reached out to him. Yet he was in a group of Christians who professed love for one another.

Recognizing that it was probably neither his shyness nor the other students' reticence that was the difficulty, where do we look for the answer? And how does one explain the presence of the Spirit of Love in such a situation? Obviously much of it has to do with the student's youth, and young people's own insecurities about themselves, and the like. But does this excuse the situation? And is this a situation restricted to young people alone?

Perhaps a partial answer may be groped at by understanding the motivations of the group for coming together in the first place. While Christian worship was certainly a core element in their motivation, a desire for companionship was probably also present. But having it present did not mean that they knew how to express it, to him at any rate.

When I talked to him another time he did admit that often there were friendly glances, timid half-smiles, none of which he picked up on. And here is where we can aid the Spirit of Love. When we are in a group, any kind of group, the awesome possibility exists that the Spirit is depending on us to make his love manifest to someone who is alone in that crowd. This does not mean, of course, that we should wander around seeking the lonely and isolated, but it does mean that we should be sensitive to another's need, and have the courage to take the first step, and then allow the Spirit to do the rest. This implies taking a risk and making ourselves vulnerable. It means that we could be rebuffed, but as people guided by a Spirit of Love, this is the task we are called to perform, because it has already been our fortunate lot to have received this love from him who loves us.

We are called into a conversion process whenever we agree to allow the Spirit to have dominance in our lives. We cannot attend a liturgy, a gathering of fellow worshipers, and choose to remain unmoved. We have to be willing to risk it; in fact entering a Christian community intrinsically implies this willingness. And what do we risk? Ourselves; all that we hold on to for security, even for identity. As Spirit directed people, we have to agree to a conversion of heart, from a self-oriented outlook to one in which the other, especially the other who is in need, can become significant.

If my friend had been absorbed into such a group, he would have been drawn out of himself and invited into a circle where the love of the Spirit would have been truly a dominant motif. And who is to say they didn't try? Perhaps it was his feelings of inadequacy that perpetuated his isolation. Perhaps if he had let the Spirit of Love work in him he would have yielded to their friendly glances with a greater ease. Whatever may have been the point remains: that where the Spirit dwells there dwells a people willing to change their outlook, from an inward focus to an other-directed focus, a focus of selfless caring and Christ-centered love.

Joy

Another change the Holy Spirit effects in prayer is joy and

happiness. Anyone who submits to the Spirit and permits him to lead experiences a changed attitude toward daily life. And this is an attitude characterized by a confident happiness that refuses to go away, even in the face of death and sorrow. It is not superficial, for it is grounded in a realization of one's true state on this earth, that of a creature dependent on a loving God for sustenance. Let me tell you of a retreatant who experienced this joy. She was a housewife, the mother of three children, and while she prayed throughout her life, she felt that her prayers lacked something. She wanted to go deeper into the world of the Spirit and permit him entrance into her life on a more intimate level. I suggested that she make a directed retreat. She agreed to it, after inquiring as to what it was all about. I told her that it was a vehicle through which her longings might become realized.

On the evening of her retreat she arrived on schedule and we got together for the first conference. I suggested that she take it easy and prepare herself for listening to the Lord by resting well and exploring her new environs. Also, I said, let's begin to enjoy the silence you are entering into, seeing it as a necessary prerequisite to listening to the Spirit. At our next conference I suggested that she continue her process of relaxing by going out to nature, allowing its beauty to seep into her soul, and relishing all as gifts from God.

She looked at me with a half-smile and a look of wonder. "You know, I used to do a lot of that when I was a kid, but recently I have been avoiding it; the beauties of nature just scare me too much. I cry a lot. It is all so beautiful." I was touched, and replied, "Well then, you are way ahead of the game; and cry as much as you want, remembering where these gifts of nature come from." She nodded in understanding and left.

When she returned the next day her account of prayer went something like this: "I did what you said, and as I looked at the things in the garden I would hear God saying to me, 'See how much I love you.' He never said it with force, just tenderly." The refrain of the day was this gentle whispering in her heart, "See how much I love you." Accompanying it was a peace and happiness. "I felt content and full," she said.

The next morning she awoke early, wanting, as she said, "to

experience a sunrise with my God." Her description of her prayer was couched in romantic terms, speaking of God as her lover, one who caressed her with the morning breeze.

I suggested that she now pray on God's forgiving love for her by reflecting on her own sins and how he has always forgiven them. I urged her to a realistic apprehension of them, allowing herself to refeel them in her heart, and then to remember the feelings accompanying the forgiveness.

The day was one of almost continuous tears. The experience of forgiveness generated strong feelings of joy, of peace and of trust. She described them: "I felt that I am his child whom he has loved so tenderly and nourished over all these years, even when I didn't realize he was around." She paused, with tears in her eyes, and then went on, "How can I be loved so completely and know this love and yet have neglected and abused it for so long?" At this point she broke down and sobbed. "I feel blessed, so extremely *blessed,*" she cried. "I just don't understand it."

The remainder of the retreat built on this, and many tears accompanied her prayer. She was also overwhelmed with peace and intense joy. On one of these latter days she saw his love as "a wind that had always been just waiting for a resting place, and now I know that I am that resting place and he is happy in me."

When she left that retreat her joy was intermingled with a deep peace. It was a realistic one as well, since she felt that never before had she confronted her sinfulness and experienced her failures as she had done in her contemplations on the retreat.

Since then she has had to endure some quite painful struggles in her life. Her youngest daughter developed an incurable disease and became, in fact, bedridden. When we talked about it the pain within her was evident, but within that pain her retreat joy perdured.

She explained it to me by saying, "I am happy. I can truthfully say that, even though I feel a part of me is dying inside. My joy comes from my retreat where I saw how much I am loved in my sins and how much he is present in my life. I know that my God has his reasons for this illness, and from him I will receive what I need to endure."

The joy that the Spirit brings lasts. I think one way of separating superficial exuberance and this gift of the Spirit is to see whether it perdures through a calamity. If it does, then the joy of the Spirit is present. Let me try to explain it further. A close friend of mine once described the fruits of this joy as something that makes a darkness gracious. It is tied up with the paschal mystery and the agony of Jesus in the garden. He suffered and really hurt intensely, to the excruciating point of bleeding all over his body, but then he submitted to the will of his Father, and the Spirit filled him with the meaning he needed to go on. Joy is knowing why you are suffering, when you do. It is the realization of a firm belief that the darkness is gracious and will eventually reveal a more abundant life.

The joy of the Spirit is clearly not the joy of a Saturday night bash. It goes far deeper, and those who submit to the Spirit, even as Jesus did, will experience the change of perception that transforms pain and failure into an Easter joy.

Peace

"Peace I bequeath to you,
my own peace I give you.
A peace the world cannot give,
this is my gift to you" (Jn. 14:27).

When Jesus promised us peace he was not speaking of the sort of peace we have come to expect from this world—that is, peace as opposed to warring conflicts. That is certainly something we must hope for, but the peace of Jesus goes far beyond this. It is also not an ebullient feeling, like the euphoria one may feel on a particularly beautiful day. Again, that too is a very pleasant experience, but it is not the peace of Jesus. Often we reduce the richness of meaning inherent in the kind of peace that the Lord brings us and consequently find ourselves let down more often than needed. For this world is often at war, be it between countries or within community or family circles. Misunderstandings and unkind actions abound; often the hoped-for sunshine does not materialize, and the day turns out gloomy and depressing. And then, far from experiencing euphoria, we feel irritability and impatience. We feel restless and out of sorts, and peace does not appear to be around. But the peace that the Spirit brings, the gift we have been promised, is far different than euphoria.

Peace has age-old connotations in the Jewish tradition. It speaks of that time when God will once again be reconciled with his people. With Jesus this reconciliation was effected, and so his first words to his apostles after his resurrection were, "Peace be with you" (Jn. 20:20). Now we have been reconciled; now we know of our destiny: union with an all-forgiving God through the blood of his Son Jesus. And this gift has now called us into an identification with the process of reconciliation initiated by the Father. Jesus follows up his greeting of peace with: "As the Father sent me so am I sending you" (Jn. 20:21). We now know what we are to be about, and in this knowledge our lives are given meaning and direction.

Peace is the gift of direction. When Jesus promised us peace, he promised us eternal life. The gift of the Spirit is the realization that our lives are not like driftwood on a mighty sea, but rather precious vessels, dearly loved and cherished by the all-good God. The peace we are gifted with is the calm knowledge of being aware of our destiny. No matter what prevails, "even if we are troubled or worried, or being persecuted, or lacking food or clothes, or being threatened or even attacked" (Rom. 8:35), we know that we will not be separated from our destiny, the love of Christ. This peace is not an ephemeral sensation that comes and goes with a person's changing moods. Rather it is an awareness in the belief that in the long run I am going somewhere, and that "somewhere" is to an inheritance of eternal life promised to us by the Lord. It asks us to put pains, trials, and failures in perspective and so endure them with peace, knowing that "these are the trials through which we triumph, by the power of him who loved us" (Rom. 8:37).

When we pray, the consquences lead us to this peace—a confident belief that our lives are going somewhere and an acceptance of difficulties as the vehicles of our victory. The consequences are exciting, and anyone who allows the Spirit entrance can expect this conversion to take place. No longer should one fear a loss of meaning, for in this peace all meaning is present. And this gift, as indeed with all the gifts, must be shared. We are called to spread the good news of Jesus' triumph to the whole world, to be peacemakers, direction-givers, to the whole world.

I remember a young man who came seeking this peace in a retreat. He felt that his life needed direction and that his marriage was suffering because of a lack of it. He believed that he ought to take a job in some capacity for the Church, be it in parish ministry or in a campus setting. But he wasn't sure, and his wife was not at all convinced that it was a good idea. He felt that a more attentive listening to the Spirit would provide him with the direction.

As we entered into the retreat I suggested that he let go of any expectations he had, except that of knowing God's will, and allow the Spirit to lead him where he chose. He was a very docile retreatant and had little difficulty settling into a series of meditations from Scripture that spoke of surrender. He knew Scripture well, and we always discussed the appropriateness of each passage before he prayed on it. Let me describe a part of the process that followed.

On the evening of the second day, we talked about his prayer —using two meditations of Psalm 131, which deals with childlike trust in God. As a backdrop to his prayer, I offered him the questions St. Paul asked after his dramatic encounter with God: "Lord, who are you?" and "Lord, what would you have me do?"

The next day he returned quite peaceful, with a feeling of being affirmed by God. I asked him to elaborate. The psalm had touched him very deeply and the questions had instilled a sense of confidence in him. He felt that he was receiving a grace of a truer perspective about things. It appeared to him that all he wanted to do was know Christ Jesus and that his other questions about his family and employment would be answered out of that. I suggested that he pray on the life of Christ, giving him passages that offered glimpses of Jesus' personality.

It was a good day for him. He came in with a sense of enthusiasm and a feeling of happiness about the way Jesus loved and about himself being loved by Jesus. He said it was the first time that he had really experienced the depth with which Jesus loved. I asked him whether he felt Jesus loved him in this way, or whether it was Jesus loving in general that excited him. "In general," he replied, "but I know he loves me a lot too."

I suggested that he divide his life up into three parts, and starting from his earliest moments recall the sins he had committed, then relive the feelings he had had on each one, the feelings after the sin, and then the experience of God's forgiveness of it. I urged him to beg God for the grace of true sorrow for his sins, and to wait silently until he felt the sorrow, as well as the subsequent forgiveness, before going on. I emphasized that this was not an exercise in cataloging his sins, but an opportunity to experience from the concreteness of his own life the ways God had loved him already.

He returned the next day calm and somewhat sad. He was amazed at what he had done in the past, but even more amazed that God had forgiven him. He was quite at peace, though, and clearly felt the authenticity of his prayer. This was not a depression of the evil spirit, but of true awareness of our sinful condition.

Then I asked him to meditate on the passion. Picture the scene at Gethsemane, I directed, and then get as close to Jesus as possible as he starts to experience his agony. Accompany him through it, watching his face, mainly his eyes, and let them speak to you. Do this throughout the passion, staying as close to Jesus as the soldiers will allow you, picturing each scene in detail as you go along, and make sure to take your time on each one. Immerse yourself not in the suffering, but in the love that called it forth.

When you get to Calvary, try to get as close to the cross as possible, together with the little group already there, and continue watching his eyes as he dies on the cross. Just before he dies he speaks to you, I went on. Listen carefully, because his words are almost inaudible. He says, "Joe, come follow me." And then he dies, and you have no chance to reply to his invitation. Stop the meditation when you get to that point, I suggested, and allow yourself to experience the emptiness in your life with Jesus dead. The next morning write a letter of response to Jesus, and then we'll get together again.

His prayer had been profound, filled with deep feelings of love and peace, of being sustained, and cherished by Jesus. It was a very personal prayer, a prayer of the heart. He had difficulty recounting it, but he gave me what I needed through tone, mood and innuendo to know that the Lord had definitely been with him. The prayers were characterized by many tears and long pauses during which he surrendered to the Spirit and didn't feel obligated to go through the respective episode of the passion he happened to be praying on. I listened in awe and commended him on his openness, particularly his flexibility in allowing the Spirit to lead him. His letter was simple and was an unequivocal "yes" to whatever God wanted from him. In it he experienced a deep sense of being specially chosen.

I suggested that he now pray on the resurrection accounts and urged him to give his letter to the risen Christ, continuing to watch Christ's face, particularly his eyes.

He returned for his next appointment deeply at peace, and very happy. There was also a new understanding of what God wanted him to do. St. Paul's questions that I had given him earlier in the retreat had surfaced, and the answers to them were both clear and ambiguous. "Follow me, and remain in my love" was paramount, but the where and the how was not forthcoming. It didn't disturb him, though, and I was at peace about it, pointing out that the Lord, in his way and in his time, would certainly reveal to him the specifics of the call.

Shortly after the retreat he called me and told me about his new job. He was working in a parish, had an excellent pastor as his boss, a man sold on team ministry, and was receiving a salary that, while not abundant, was also far more than he had expected. His wife still didn't approve of his choice of profession, but appeared to be accepting it more because she saw it as something he needed to do for himself. She had also told him that since he looked so much happier now she had no intention of complaining about the small salary. When I asked him whether he was at peace about it, he replied, "Definitely, though I know it is going to be a rough road financially, especially as our kids start getting older."

His life was going to have its difficulties, as is true with most of us, but armed with the conviction that he was living out the destiny God had invited him to, he was at peace. It is this gift that the Spirit gives us, and when received in faith it will enable us to endure the trials to come, confident that it is through them that we will triumph.

Patience

The Oxford English Dictionary defines patience as "the suffering or enduring (of pain, trouble or evil) with calmness and composure." It is further described as "a quiet or self-possessed waiting for something.'' Patience all too often conjures up the image of a meek and docile housewife who puts up with every indignity with a long-suffering and stoic acceptance of her life of servitude as the natural order of things. In contrast, impatience recalls to mind a chafing person always on the verge of muttering or gesturing harshly to express some displeasure.

While these may be popular images of patience and impatience, the *gift of patience* goes far deeper than a certain mode of behavior. The Christian who is patient has become steeped in the mystery of God's redemptive story. It seems that patience is something one has to freely choose to accept like all the other gifts. It is an active response to an invitation by God to become involved with his mystery, and a willingness to believe that we are destined for a greatness that puts the honors and privileges of this world in their proper place. I think that patience speaks of true perspective, of a life lived in this world but with eyes always directed toward a glory to come. The acceptance of trials with courage and fortitude, then, is not done for stoic reasons, or because of one's own helplessness to change things. Rather patience is a recognition of the truth that through the acceptance of trials one is freely choosing to accept God's redemptive story. It is a willingness to see oneself caught up in the paschal mystery of birth-death-resurrection so as to be caught up with the glory that God has promised us.

But is this acceptance a passive surrendering to the powers of this world, with all its injustices and hatred? Is it a dismal hope that somehow God will reward one for putting up with one's sorrow because I am ''offering it up'' to him? Does resignation imply that we are to sit around and allow evil to triumph in a chimeric hope that all will turn out well in the end? Hardly! This is not the gift of the Spirit. In fact it could be the following of the path of least resistance.

Patience, when received and accepted, puts our story with God's story. And his story is one of life, and life more abundant. We become partners with him and choose to work with him to make this more abundant life possible for all people. So when we see signs of lesser life we must reach out to try to effect greater life in that situation.

Anyone who receives this gift of patience cannot ignore injustice, cannot let the sinful ways of the world endure, cannot refuse to give a cup of water to one who is thirsty. Patience is active; it joins our story with Christ's story of redemption so that in partnership the life, the abundant life, that God has earned for us may be realized.

The gift of patience often can be manifested by impatience with this world that has yet to hear of the good news of redemption. Once a retreatant told me his story of struggle in the battle against injustice. In his country persecution of Christians had been going on for some years. The government was very anxious to maintain control of most of the country's economy by keeping the land under the ownership of a very few landowners. They were all high positioned members of the government, and they propagated themselves effectively.

All was well until the Church started rebelling against this unjust state of affairs. Then persecution started, at first subtly but before long with greater overtness. My retreatant was in the midst of the struggle from the very beginning and had just been released from jail after eighteen months of imprisonment. The atrocities that went on within those prison walls were endured by his fellow political prisoners—half of them priests and men and women religious—through long periods of daily prayer. He told me that he had seldom experienced the power of a praying community as much as he did during those months of torment. "I will never forget the courage and fortitude those prayers brought me that morning when I was being 'interrogated,' " he said, smiling ruefully and showing me burn marks on his arm, hidden under his shirt sleeve. "It was the one source of consolation I had, knowing that I was a part of something much bigger than just me, that I was tied up with God's redemptive work. That's what gave me the courage to endure. And I felt a power inside me that seemed to blind out all the pain."

This account illustrates well, I believe, the consequences of accepting the Spirit's gift of patience. To be a Spirit-motivated person means that we cannot take injustice or any other signs of evil lying down. It means that we cannot ignore our brother or sister in need but must reach out to that person so that God's story of redemptive love may be that much more manifest on earth. Patience gives us hope to persevere as we struggle against sins within ourselves, and in the world around us, for it gifts us with the true perspicuity for this work seen always in the light of that glory to come in the next.

A Kind Goodness

We long for a goodness within ourselves that can be expressed in kind deeds. All of us wish that we could be genuinely concerned for our neighbor and feel disappointment within ourselves when we are not. Together with St. Paul we often mutter our confusion, noting that "I cannot understand my own behavior. I fail to carry out the things I want to do, and I find myself doing the very things I hate" (Rom. 7:15). We pray for the graces we need to be generous and kind toward people, but, let's face it, often we are anything but generous. We are not only without kindness but with a lot of antagonism. And as much as we try, we secretly believe that we will never really love our neighbor the way we are supposed to, the way Jesus does.

Kindness speaks of belonging to a family, to a group, of being kin with someone. It speaks not so much of gestures as a state of being in a belonging stance with another. In this gift we are offered kinship with God, and by that relationship we understand that all people are our brothers and sisters. Being kind to a stranger is being kind to our brother or sister. And this means that in some way we are being good to ourselves, because we all belong to one family, with God as our Father.

It is out of this belief that we choose to be kin with our neighbor: because God has already chosen to be kin with us. And the Spirit of God has to first touch our hearts with this gift before we can hope to go out to another in kinship.

The call to convert to his kinship with us must first be responded to before we can hope to reach out to others. Without God our efforts would lack authenticity, for who among us does not carry a selfish streak that whispers inside, "Let's see what I can get out of this one, brother or not"? To subvert this we need to allow the Spirit prior entrance into our hearts and to permit him to gift us with kinship in his family, his own family.

This means making ourselves vulnerable to the Spirit. It means allowing him to surface for us things about ourselves that are not so good, not so kind. We need to face the darkness within so that God's light may become ours in the truth that that confrontation will bring. I think that unless we face up to the hostile manipulative part of ourselves we will not be able to plumb the depths of goodness that are within us. We need to experience our own poverty and indigence. We must be honest with ourselves and admit our helplessness to love as Jesus loves without his altruistic Spirit within us. This is hard for us to do, for we really believe that we have a lot of goodness to offer, and the fact that it is unappreciated is "their" fault, not ours. To strip ourselves of this is a task that will take a lifetime to realize, but the Spirit calls us to make this change in our lives. The more we change our inflated self-concepts the more the Spirit will fill us with his love, and armed with that we can go out to our brothers and sisters and be confidently good, genuinely kind to them. Not that *we* bring about the change. What happens, it seems to me, is that we begin to recognize our own helplessness to change, and in the poverty of that knowledge, we present ourselves to the Spirit who will then gladly effect the change in us. This is the conversion to the Spirit's love for us: to recognize our emptiness and beg that the Spirit's gifts fill us with his selfless goodness in rearing us as brothers and sisters of one family. It happens in prayer, over a lifetime.

I remember an old friend of mine, since deceased, who ruefully commented to me one day that after fifty years of religious life he felt that he had regressed to pre-novitiate days in kindness to his neighbor. I asked him what he meant, somewhat surprised at his comment, especially since I esteemed him highly and many thought of him as a man close to God. "Well," he went on, "I feel that I am becoming more of a sinner than I was in my youth. It seems that I get angry more, am far more impatient than ever before, and am lacking in tolerance to all kinds of people who previously I found quite tolerable. I know a lot of it is old age, but I would have imagined that by now all my life's prayers would have more than compensated for that." He looked at me and smiled, then went on. "I guess I'll have to leave my senile failures up to God's mercy," he said.

But the truth of the matter was that he was one of the most generous people I've known. His kindness extended to all kinds of people, and he seldom allowed inconvenience to get in the way of helping another. Not only did he always help when he could, but he often went out of his way to offer a hand, and no task was too menial for him to tackle.

I told him this, and I assured him that as far as I was concerned he was one of the finest examples of Christian kindness I've known. He smiled again, then said, "Thank you, but I have a long way to go." It's been some years now since that conversation, but somehow I can never forget it. The humility that was so unassuming, and the need he expressed for God to fill him, remain as examples of that true perspective all of us are called to maintain. Throughout his life he had been open to his own inadequacies in prayer, and in return the Spirit's gifts of kindness and genuine goodness emanated from him in an effortless flow of actions for his neighbor that did not cease till his death. That he didn't know it was a sure mark of his sanctity. In that ignorance he knew the truth about himself and about God's power working in him.

To be a good Christian means caring for others because you belong to them, as a member of that family which calls God, "Abba, Father." It means that a good action toward another is done because that other is a part of you—is your brother or sister, your kin. When you know your kin you know who comes first in your life; you know who receives your goodness. In a Christian context this means the world. It is to the whole world that we are called to be good. The thought is as magnanimous as the gift, and it is up to us to make this gift a living reality.

Trust

To trust someone is to believe in that person. It calls forth a willingness to put into practice the faith we *say* we have in someone. It urges us to let go of our doubts and give another the respect of believing in his or her own prowess. When it comes to God the same letting-go is involved. We are called to believe in God's prowess to save us and to heal our wounds and anxieties. Trust calls us to believe in the faith we claim to possess, not through words but through actions. As the commercial says, "Put your money where your mouth is."

But faith does not happen in a vacuum. It is a gift of the Holy Spirit, and as with all gifts it can be rejected. The only way we can increase our confidence in the gift is through regular contact with the giver. We need assurances that the giver is trustworthy. When it comes to God, these assurances can occur only if we go to him in prayer and allow him to show us how trustworthy he really is. "Have patience; things will work out—I promise you," says the Lord to our hearts. When we believe this and face our trial with renewed hope, then the gift of trust has once again been received from the Holy Spirit, and once again we find the courage to go on. This is the conversion that the Spirit offers us: to believe and to endure trustingly, whatever comes, because we know that our God is good and "takes no pleasure in abasing and afflicting the human race" (Lam. 3:33).

One who submits oneself to prayer submits oneself to a life of hope. It is a trust that daily becomes reaffirmed as daily the prayer reveals the reason for it. Once I had a retreatant who was very anxious about her next assignment. She was a religious, and even though she had been one for many years she was not able to resign herself to it. She was filled with anxiety and fantasized the worst possible assignment for herself, allowing desolation over the fantasy to overwhelm her. On the retreat her meditations were fraught with these distractions; the evil spirit was having a field day with her soul. In fact, she told me as much. She wished she could do something about it.

I suggested she set aside Scripture for a while and pray the prayer of silence. I told her to go into the chapel and, after assuming any posture she chose, just to surrender herself to the Lord, saying either the Jesus Prayer or whatever else came to her mind. I urged that she keep her words down to not more than one phrase or sentence, repeating it over and over rather than doing a lot of talking. "The point is to experience your helplessness in getting rid of this temptation," I said. "As with any temptation, all we can do is identify it as evil, beg the Lord to take it away, and then wait patiently. Sitting there in silence, experiencing your helplessness rather than just saying it, is an excellent way of inviting the Spirit into your soul."

It was a struggle. The first hour of silence was anything but silent. A thousand and one distractions kept her mind seething with activity. But she persevered, and she repeatedly told the Lord that she surrendered to him—even though she was not feeling the surrender at that point. Her second hour continued the struggle, but, perhaps because of sheer exhaustion, the turmoil appeared to be lessening. She kept up her words of surrender, uttering them less frequently and beginning to feel them more in her heart. She didn't make her third hour until late at night. As she walked into the chapel she felt a warmth within her. As she settled down to pray, it increased. She started feeling engulfed in a peace and trust in the Lord that was a wholly new experience for her. She sat very still and allowed the mood to engulf her. She hardly whispered any words, feeling the surrender that was taking place rather than uttering it.

At our next conference the gentle tranquility she was exuding clearly indicated that the Spirit had once again entered a soul and dwelt within her. She told me in a few words that it no longer mattered where she was sent and wished only that the deep feelings of trust she was now experiencing would perdure.

The Spirit visits us and changes our hearts if we but let him. He is, in fact, eager to bring us the peace that a trust in him can effect. It is a trust that does not go away, for intrinsic to it is his gift of perseverance. When we trust a human being or a human institution there is often a justifiable suspicion, bred from fear of being let down, that it may not quite work out. But once we trust in the Spirit and experience the depth of his love for us we become a resigned people, confident that our God is a God worthy of our trust.

One who begins trusting the Spirit at the present moment is a person who has agreed to start remembering the many evidences of God's fidelity through time. And the more one starts remembering, the more one's anxieties are calmed. "I will set up my dwelling among you, and I will not cast you off. I will live in your midst; I will be your God and you shall be my people. It is I, Yahweh your God, who have brought you out of the land of Egypt so that you should be their servants no longer. I have broken the yoke that bound you and have made you walk with head held high" (Lev. 26: 11-13).

The gift of trust in God is the gift of memory. We are given the chance to remember once again that our God does not let his people down and that over and over he has broken the yokes that bound us. Repeatedly he has enabled us to walk again with heads held high when we thought that our shame was too great to bear. When we trust, we recognize that our God has proven himself to us again and again, not just in salvation history but in our personal lives as well. In this gift we are called to recognize this fidelity, and by so doing we confidently trust him once again.

Gentleness

In the gift of gentleness the Spirit offers us an opportunity to touch the very core of our humanity. I feel that a gentle person is a person deeply and experientially aware of sin and failure in the personal history of his life. Gentleness is a consequence of true knowledge of oneself as sinner, forgiven over and over again by a God who does not permit failure to stand in the way of love. By wiping out that failure in repeated gestures of forgiveness God allows his love to be revealed. A person who is well aware of this, who knows of his Father's forgiveness, is a gentle person. That person knows that unworthiness, that sin—in all its many manifestations and disguises—is a part of humanity. There is little pride in gentle people, and all their dealings with others reveal this. The gentle know of their true states. They know that there is little to be proud of, little to boast about. Hence the gentle are unpretentious and always ready to listen to another's opinion, to another's anguish or hurt. A gentle person does not judge, knowing that judgment is not in his domain. He is an accepting person, who respects another's stance or contention without feeling the compulsion to degrade it.

When one enters prayer and invites the Spirit to enter in, one is inviting truth—truth about oneself, about the true state of one's soul, about awareness of sin in one's life, and about forgiveness of that sin. Gentleness, as the consequence of being aware of sin forgiven, is a gift that evolves out of this awareness.

It is a process, like all the other gifts, that lasts throughout one's life, and inherent in it is the invitation to be truly free. For a person forgiven is a person freed, and a person who is free, deeply free in one's heart, can reach out with greater ease to touch a broken heart, because that person knows brokenness and can with a greater authenticity bind up the wounds of the fallen. It generates empathy, this gift of gentleness, an involvement with another that identifies with that person's failure, not from any stance of superiority but from a stance of brotherly love.

Once a retreatant of mine, well versed in the spiritual life, gave in to various distractions during his retreat and found that his knowledge of the mechanics of prayer and the like helped him not one whit as he allowed his retreat "to fall apart," as he said. He experienced two predominant frustrations out of this: an inability to focus in on God alone, and a real sense of helplessness in extricating himself from the state of discombobulation in which he felt himself. He felt angry with himself and resented the fact that he had succumbed to temptations that he could have spotted a mile away if he had seen them in another.

When he returned to prayer he picked up St. Paul's letters and was drawn to two phrases that appeared to bring some peace to his distraught soul. One was "I want you to be happy, always happy in the Lord," and the other spoke of the Spirit of Truth. He felt an inner tugging to dwell on them at some length, and with no apparent connection he drifted into a calmness that in turn gave rise to a prayer of the imagination. He had an image of surrendering his distractions and his anger to the Lord, and he felt as if he was letting go of a support that had held him secure at the edge of a precipice. He went on to explain what followed: "As I fell, there appeared an immense green velvet cloth, billowy and caressing, and as my fall picked up momentum I felt enfolded in it with a great sensation of softness overcoming me. Gradually my fall was slowed down until I was laid safely and quite unhurt at the bottom of the cliff. I lay there content and peaceful, the feelings of anger and frustration all but gone."

From this prayer he went into a realistic series of meditations on his sins, beginning with the ways he had permitted distractions to interfere with the beginning of his retreat. The meditations were terrible struggles where he had vivid and painful recollections of his sins, mixed with many distractions. He was filled with anger and frustration and begged the Lord for forgiveness. Each time he asked he felt a momentary peace, but then he was returned to viewing his own sins again. However, each time the peace returned it was more realistic, a sense of being loved accompanying it.

Let me describe in some detail one of these episodes. He saw himself in a lighted circle, very much like the stage in a theatre-in-the-round. It was dark all around him, and he perceived the darkness to be hostile. He told himself that, for those who believe, the darkness is benevolent, but he violently reacted to that, shrieking an obscenity into the darkness in denial. Yet as he denied it a fear overtook him, for he felt wild dogs out there straining to come into his circle of light and attack him. Then he looked down and found that not only was he under the spotlight, but he was naked under the spotlight. He was reduced to utter fear and found himself trembling. Then the voice came back saying, "The darkness is benevolent." And at that moment the lights in the darkness came up a bit and he saw the dim outline of a theatre-in-the-round. "And it was filled with people praying and crying, and feeling for me." He paused, evidently moved by the memory, and then went on: "Then, suddenly, it was dark again and the voice returned telling me that the darkness was benevolent, that I should surrender to it, that in it was my Lord. And the Lord said, 'Yes, I am in the darkness, and I care dearly for you. I love you.' At that moment," he went on, "I just found myself letting go, and letting go, until a stillness filled me and I cried inside. Then the lights came up again just a little and I saw that the theatre was empty except for one seat. In it sat Jesus, abused, beaten and scourged, crowned with thorns, mocked and spat upon. And he was crying for me. I ran to him and hugged him, and cried and cried, feeling profound peace in his bloody arms."

By now the person who had been so distraught and angry with himself a few short days ago was no longer in evidence. He said that he was far calmer than he had been in years, and the violence that was within him was giving way to a new sensation, "a feeling of firm gentleness." It was built on in his subsequent prayer periods. One of these contemplations occurred as follows.

He had read a brief chapter in a book on the Lamb of God. That triggered it. "Suddenly," he said, "I put the book down and saw the Lamb filled with glory, regal and content, happy about me, and happy with me. I felt wave after wave of peace and was led to the Book of Revelation. I felt quietly awestruck at the image of the Lamb. I cried tears of joy and over and over again thanked the Lamb, embracing him. He turned toward me and licked me, tenderly, with affection. He licked me again and again. I saw the new Jerusalem. I saw the branding iron of love. It said 'God alone' and the Lamb imprinted it upon my forehead. There was a light around me but no warmth, warmth but no heat. I thanked him again and again in my utter helplessness to respond to such a love. And then he, the Lamb, thanked me. He thanked me for letting him love me. I felt him say: "No more tears or mourning, for the world of the past has gone, and no more guilt or sadness; but delight in me, the Lamb of God who licks you tenderly."

When he left the retreat he felt humbler than he had felt in years. He had experienced failure, had been repulsed by his sins, and had been lifted out of them by actions of the Spirit that were quite "other," not directly related to anything he had done. He had felt his helplessness, and many times he had experienced the poverty of his condition. He left aware of God's forgiving love. He left as a gentle person, humbled by his sins, and by the special graces he had received from the Lord.

Self-Control

Of the gifts of the Holy Spirit listed by St. Paul in his Letter to the Galatians self-control is outlined for us in greatest detail. St. Paul lists many of the consequences of not having self-control. Accordingly, it is a relatively simple thing to infer what the signs of this gift are, for they would be the other side of "fornication, gross indecency, sexual irresponsibility, idolatry and sorcery; feuds and wrangling, jealousy, bad temper and quarrels; disagreements, factions, envy, drunkenness, orgies and similar things" (Gal. 5:19–20). He goes on to say, "You cannot belong to Christ Jesus unless you crucify all self-indulgent passions and desires" (Gal. 5:24). The difficulty arises in that we do have self-indulgent passions and desires. As much as we long to be the ideal Christian, loving one another as Christ loves us, we love not as he loves but as we love, which includes a lot of selfishness, uncontrolled passion and self-seeking gratification.

Does this mean that we do not receive this gift, in a lasting manner at any rate? Does it mean that we do not belong to Christ Jesus no matter how much we may want to? No. We long for self-control in our lives, and our failures in achieving control do not indicate a failure to want it.

It seems that the gift of self-control lies in this desire— to *want* the chasteness that belonging to Jesus calls us to receive. Self-control is the yearning we have for a life of single-mindedness and centrality of vision that has Jesus and his selfless way of loving as the sole motivator of our every action. It is the vow of chastity that we are all called to make as Christ-followers and children of a loving Father. For chastity is a call to a single-minded devotion to the Lord our God. He becomes the center, he is the prime focus, and all else gets arranged around him. To be chaste is to be almost like the mad scientist who locks himself in his laboratory poring over one thing and one thing only—his scientific experiments. Nothing else matters but his work, and that alone motivates his every action. This is the sort of single-mindedness we are called to receive in the gift of self-control—without the eccentricities of the mad scientist, of course, but certainly with his drive and determination, with his devotion to one thing in life. God is this pivotal vision for us. In chastity we receive the gift of perceiving this truth and allowing this perspective to be the one that propels our daily lives, distracted and unchaste as they are, toward him.

But self-control as the gift of a central vision of God is hardly attainable in this life, no matter how much we may work at it. In fact there are many motivators that guide our actions, and seldom are our actions as purely Christ-motivated as we would like them to be. More often than not the motivations are selfish in some way or other. While they may be honorable, they are but slightly of God. Does this mean that self-control for chaste living is a gift given in small amounts? I don't think so. It is a gift that accepts this centrality of vision and imprints in our hearts the desire for it. The gift is to *want* chasteness, to yearn for a purity of heart that belonging to Jesus implies. But it is not *just* wanting it. It is also that willingness to take steps to do something about becoming, in a slow, often painful process, the perfect Christian Jesus has called us to be—in fact, to strive after the impossible ideal of being perfect even as our

Father in heaven is perfect. The very thought sounds blasphemous, except that Jesus himself spoke of it to us. He believes we can do it, and the Spirit's gift offers us the desire to realize this ambitious ideal. Let me tell you four short stories about this gift and its consequences.

Once a retreatant told me of a physically intimate relationship he was having with one of his students. He was a college professor working with graduate students, and the woman, about his age and unmarried, shared his own academic interests. But he was a religious, and had been one for quite some years. The relationship had caused him intense anguish and many tears but without affording a solution. He felt trapped, for he firmly believed that he had a religious vocation, but at the same time felt helpless to effect any change in the state of things. He was seeing me almost as a last resort before making a decision to leave religious life. He was very open about it all and said that he felt a need to tell me all about it at the very beginning as a sign of his willingness to be open to the Lord and his graces. I listened closely, aware that here was evidence of the Spirit working already in the desire to be open and honest, and indeed in the fact that he was talking to someone about it.

I thanked him for trusting me with his story and pointed out the Spirit's grace already at work in this. I suggested that we set aside the problem for the moment, conscious of it but not "working on it" directly. The point was God's love for us. Once that was experienced, then all else, including the problem, would be set in a proper perspective. The healing would follow. He agreed to the approach and left in a relatively tranquil state to pray on the words of the prophet Isaiah:

> Do not be afraid, for I have redeemed you;
> I have called you by your name, you are mine.
> Should you pass through the sea, I will be with you;
> or through rivers, they will not swallow you up.
> Should you walk through fire, you will not be scorched
> and the flames will not burn you.
> For I am Yahweh, your God,
> the Holy One of Israel, your Savior. . . .
> Because you are precious in my eyes,
> because you are honored, and I love you . . . (Is. 43:2–4).

On the following day he returned much at peace and miraculously, as he told me, undistracted by his problem.

The process that followed was one in which the Lord showed him in various ways that he was loved and respected just as he was, with his problem, with his weaknesses. Now this, I believe, is an instance of the gift of self-control at work. It was a gentle recognition of God loving him no matter what and an accompanying desire on his part to respond to that love and that love alone.

Toward the end of the retreat I brought up his problem. He was quite at peace by this time and appeared almost as if he had forgotten about it. I said, "Do you know that the Lord is calling you to let go of your relationship—in the intimate way it exists, at any rate?" He looked up and stared hard at me. "Yes," he said and then broke down sobbing. He wept for a long time. Finally he got up without a word and left the room.

The next day ended his retreat. In our last conference I emphasized that he now had to act; the relationship had to end as it was then lived out. He left with a firm decision to end it, and in fact to break off all contact with her, for a while anyway.

He called me a few days later. The woman, even though she was supporting him and praying with him on his retreat, was thoroughly torn up—understandably so. However she had agreed to abide by whatever decision he came to on the retreat and was willing to go through with a separation.

But they didn't. It was too hard to end things just like that. He modified his earlier decision and did what he believed seemed right. They did not end things immediately but definitely began modifying some of their behavior that went against his deepest convictions. I supported him and promised that I would be with them in prayer.

In the next few months they went through plenty of struggles trying to find ways of simply being friends and not lovers. Finally, after over a year, they both arrived at a point where in their hearts they knew it was over. In an extraordinarily painful session the decision was finally made, with a finality they both felt in their hearts, and they left each other, promising prayers and love for always.

Yet it didn't end there. They continued on a very infrequent basis to see one another. Then other interests—a job for her in another city, a new assignment for him—gradually ended their relationship, and the correspondence they initially sustained has now all but evaporated.

The gift of self-control is the gift of first wanting, and then doing something about, God as one's central vision. In this story it is evident that it comes to us in a process in which a gradual transformation of oneself occurs. And often it occurs with pain and many tears.

The Lord gives us the desire for a chaste life in many ways. Sometimes it comes through a process of discernment as I have just described; at other times the gift occurs in a far more dramatic way. Let me tell you another story where this gift is seen at work.

It was 2:30 in the morning when the phone rang. A friend of mine had just found her friend and neighbor heavily drugged and in an almost comatose state in his house. She was near hysteria and had no idea what to do. Could I get over there right away. "Why me?" I asked. "He needs a doctor." "No," she screamed. "He's asking for a priest. Come now. He may go at any minute." "O.K.," I said, and hung up.

When I got to his house and was shown into the kitchen where he lay on the floor, I was shocked. The place was a mess, but worse still, there was no furniture in the house. He was lying motionless, with his eyes distended. I found the phone and called the suicide hotline. I explained the situation, and they guided me in the slow process of bringing him around.

I had never met him before, but over the next three days, as I talked to him almost constantly, following what I had been instructed to do, I got to know him quite well. His story was incredible. He seemed to have done everything in his life. He had been a violinist, a pilot in the navy, a medical student for three years, and now was a commercial pilot for a major airline. It was because of medical training that he knew exactly the right combination of drugs to take. The doctor on the hotline told me, after I had found out what drugs he had taken, that it had been a lethal dosage, and he really didn't know why he was still alive. The first task I had was to talk him into going to the hospital. After several hours he agreed, assuring me that the only reason he was going was that I was a priest.

The rest of the recovery proceeded without complications. He had tried to kill himself because his live-in girlfriend had gone off with another man, taking their furniture with her. The consequence was his suicide attempt.

As he continued recovering I asked him why he wanted a priest and not a doctor when he was on the verge of death. "Because I felt a need for love," he said, "and a longing to be forgiven. I don't know where it came from, but that's all I knew I needed before I died." He paused. "I used to be a good Christian—Mass every Sunday, confessions every other week, the whole bit—but all that was a long time ago."

He turned and faced me. Tears were welling up in his eyes. "I want to change," he said. "I want to love God and become more like him, but I don't know how to do it." He was silent and looked away for a while. Then, still looking away, he said, "Will you help me?" "Of course," I replied. He beckoned me over to his bed and gave me a long embrace.

The gift of self-control, it seems to me, is this gift of wanting to be holy, longing to be better, and it is especially vivid in a situation like this, where out of total failure, to the point of death, there arose the stirrings in a heart for love and for forgiveness, and an accompanying cry for help.

The third episode again illustrates the Spirit's gift, and again points to self-control more as something we long for and seek to achieve than something already given, once and for all. The conversion is to want it, and the wanting can often exist for a long time before anything is done about it. It happens though, eventually, for those who pray in faith, believing that the holiness of God is theirs freely given, always available.

He was a tall man, but he gave the appearance of smallness. When he first came into my office he seemed to be cowering. He was slightly stooped and, though in his late twenties, was balding rapidly. I invited him to sit down. Since this was a first interview, I invited him to begin by sharing with me some basics about his prayer life. He answered quite amiably although he had a lisp in his speech that made me strain to hear him. He was a nominal Christian, one who attended Mass with some frequency but did not always make it every week. He was married and had one child. Being a long distance truck driver, he was often away from home for weeks on end. It was a rough life but he enjoyed the outdoors and did not mind it too much.

The difficulty he was having, he told me, was with his family. "Raising a kid these days," he said, "is very hard, especially when you are on the road so much. Often I come home very tired and wanting to just have some beers and go to bed. But I find it impossible to do, for the kid starts interrupting me and wanting my attention. And the wife doesn't help me at all. She appears to encourage him in fact, and if I didn't do something about it I would have no peace at all."

I nodded in understanding. "What seems to be the problem?" I asked. "Well, I'm not a very religious man," he went on, "but God is important to me, and what he thinks about me matters. And I feel that I let God down when I'm at home in that I have real problems controlling my family, especially my kid." He hastened to add, "Now mind you, I don't play around when I'm on the road, though I have many chances to do so. I really love my wife and want to be always faithful to her. The other truckers make fun of me at times because I don't join them when I go out at night to get some fun. But I'm serious about my marriage and don't intend messing it up."

I smiled in encouragement and then urged him to tell me about his son. "Well," he went on, "I don't claim to know much about raising a kid, but I tell you it's a tough job. Often I have to discipline him to get him to shut up and to keep away from me when I'm tired and just want to be left alone." "What do you do to him?" I asked, beginning to suspect something. "Well, I take my belt to him," he said, "and give him a good thrashing. That shuts him up, especially the times when he passes out after I've beaten him." "He what?" I asked with some alarm. "Well, yeah," he went on, "that's what bugs me. Sometimes he just passes out on me. In fact my wife has had to take him to the hospital a few times." "Does she try to stop you?" I asked. "Yes," he replied, "but I'm so mad at him that I shove her off and keep on beating him." Trying to keep my mounting anger down, I asked him whether he punished him in any other way. He replied, "Oh, sure, sometimes I just don't let him have any dinner, but force him to drink some hot sauce straight from the bottle. He throws up after that and has gotten pretty sick a few times, but I do it for his own good. I've got to teach him respect for his elders." "But you don't feel so good about it before God, do you?" I asked. "Well, that's the thing," he went on. "I feel that I get too violent with him at times, and God may punish me for it." "How about your wife?" I asked. "What does she say?" "Well, she has warned me not to be so rough with him, especially since he now never comes close to me when I get home, and in fact runs away and hides from me. She has told me he cries in his sleep every night and he could be getting sick or something."

I imagined the poor child to be about nine or ten years old, but thought that I had better get an accurate fix on his age. Therefore I asked him how old his boy was. His answer really bowled me over. I just felt a numb fear for the boy and immense sympathy for him. He was two and a half years old!

I decided to talk to him sternly. I told him that what he was doing was extremely serious, and that if he wanted God to help him he would first have to make up his mind to stop beating his son. "The spiritual direction starts here," I said, "with firmly deciding to change your behavior. You must start controlling yourself." I talked in this vein a long time, using repetitive statements to emphasize the seriousness of the situation. I pointed out that his son was not common property to be beaten up and thrown around at will but rather a precious gift from God for him to love and cherish. "If it has not happened already, your son will begin to hate you," I said. "You have to promise me that you will stop hitting him or punishing him in any way." He agreed, somewhat cowed. I demanded that he go to a marriage counselor or a psychiatrist, emphasizing the point that I believed he needed help that I was unable to give. I pointed out that normal fathers don't do this to their kids. He agreed, and as he left I assured him that he was welcome to return and see me anytime, but that I would give him a hard time unless I saw some changes in the treatment of his son. "If you keep up your present behavior," I concluded, "you may have a murder charge on your hands, and the victim will be your own son." He got up, promised me that he would make an appointment with a psychiatrist as soon as he got home, and shuffled out of my office.

He called me some weeks later. He was now seeing a psychiatrist regularly and feeling the beginnings of a new confidence emerging. He asked whether he could also receive spiritual direction on an ongoing basis. I agreed, and we set up our first appointment. The process that followed gave rise to several changes in his life. First, he started a regular program of prayer. He found the long hours of driving an excellent time for meditation. Then, with the help of various psychological tools he received from his psychiatrist, he started changing his behavior at home. His wife began accompanying him when he went to see his doctor. She also prayed with him when he was home. And his son did not cry as much anymore. Needless to say, the psychological scars on the child most certainly would need later tending, but for now the gift of self-control his father was receiving safeguarded him from physical scars.

The gift of self-control occurs whenever someone receives the motivation and acts with courage to effect a change for the better. It is seldom a *fait accompli* but often occurs in such a gradual way that it is only with hindsight that one perceives its effect. And when the change is finally accomplished the gift continues, sustaining the day-to-day activities of one's life, working in the hearts of those who want it. This next episode further illustrates this point.

He was a big man, well built, and with a pleasant disposition. After talking about various inconsequential things he paused and looked at me thoughtfully. Then, as if he had just made a decision to go ahead and tell me about it anyway, he proceeded with his story.

He was a "good" Christian. He went to Mass weekly, believed in the teachings of the Church and did his best to follow them. He prayed regularly for help but had not succeeded in overcoming "it." Not wanting to push him, but needing to know what the "it" was, I asked him to elaborate.

In his work he travels a lot, he went on, and often he finds himself in a strange city after a hard day's work on the road, far away from family and home. He gets very lonely, and invariably ends up at a bar where he sits drinking alone till his roving eyes find a woman in a like predicament. From then on it's the stereotype of the "bar pick-up routine." The morning after he is filled with guilt and remorse, and he fears returning to his family. He has no one to talk to, since he can't go to his priest who has known the family for years, and he feels that the frequency of his adulterous actions has placed him far from God's love. He had not gone to Communion in over a year, and he feared the bad example he was giving his son. "Please help me," he ended. "I hate myself."

As I was listening I found myself feeling sorry for him and wanting to assure him of God's forgiveness. But that was premature. So I asked him a few questions. I wanted to get him comfortable talking to me about his pain, for I needed more information on his difficulty. Therefore I asked him how often he did the bar scene. He replied, "Seventy-five to a hundred times or so this past year." With a wry smile he added, "It's not very difficult to pick someone up if you really want to." I nodded. Then, after a pause, I said, "Why do you do it?" "Because I'm lonely, I guess. You may not believe this, but the last thing in this world I want to do is to be unfaithful to my wife, and to God. Yet I can't seem to be able to help myself. I feel that all my Christian upbringing has been made a mockery of, and that God must hate me for what I'm doing."

I was grateful that he was talking, and I prayed while I listened that the Spirit would give me what I needed to help him. He had not been able to talk to any priest about this before. He wouldn't even consider going to a psychiatrist or counselor. As far as he was concerned this was strictly in the realm of the spiritual life and had nothing to do with anything else. It was a moral problem, and in his mind that belonged to the spiritual sphere.

When he had finished he had tears in his eyes. I started by assuring him that taking the step to come in and talk about it was a very significant one and promising him God's forgiveness for his infidelities. But just being forgiven isn't enough, I went on. "We have a real problem here, and we must not brush it aside and pretend that it is going away on its own." I pointed out that many people travel on business but don't become unfaithful to their wives, and to themselves, when they feel lonely on those journeys. "Besides, you have gotten into the habit of doing it now. If you are sincere about wanting to change we are going to have to do something more than just seek the sacrament of reconciliation."

He interrupted me here, assuring me that he definitely wanted to change, and that this was why he had come. Anything I suggested he would follow. I asked him to listen again to what he just said. "You said that you are open to anything I suggest," I told him. "Well, I suggest that what I can do is confront the problem and with the grace of God forgive you your sins. Also, in the future when you are lonely, don't go into a bar where you are asking for trouble. Use the phone. Call your wife and tell her about your loneliness. And this I promise you: I will be your friend no matter what happens to you in the future. Know that you can come and talk to me or call me at any time."

His face lit up. And then he broke into tears—many, many tears that welled up from years of guilt and loneliness. When he had finished I went on: "There is a condition, though. I want to ask you to do something that I consider essential for you to kick the habit." He looked up, eyes glistening with tears, and nodded. "I want you to seek out a psychologist and follow his advice." Recalling his earlier contemptuous tones when speaking of psychiatrists, I expected a battle. I was not wrong, He shook his head very emphatically and refused. "Anything else, yes," he said, "but not that. I don't trust them one bit. I don't think I need any of their kind of help anyway. If I can just come and talk to you periodically, that will do."

I listened and then said, "I told you that I'd be your friend. Well, why don't you let me?" He looked at me quizzically. I went on, "There is a certain point that I can go to. Beyond that I am incompetent. I feel we have reached that point. I am not a psychologist, and I feel that your difficulty goes beyond the moral sphere and over into the psychological. I want you healed. I want you to be happy because that is what God wants for you. You say you are serious about being sorry for your sins. Well, prove it. Go to the psychologist, get tested, and follow his recommendation."

He was listening to me intently. After I had finished, he was silent for a long time. Then he said, "Do you know of one?"

I breathed a sign of relief. "Yes, I do, and I'll be happy to put you in touch with him. He is eminently trustworthy, he is very competent, and he will be happy to help."

He nodded, then broke down and sobbed in relief and in sorrow. Before he left he gave me a warm embrace accompanied by profuse thanks.

I saw him some months later. He looked so different from when I last saw him. He looked carefree, younger, and had a certain buoyancy in his step. He told me about it. He had first started going to daily Mass. No matter where he was he found the church and went to Mass. Next, he had gotten the help we had talked about. It was effective. No longer was he out of control, he told me. "I feel so free, oh, so free." And he grinned happily.

Self-control is the gift that is the propelling force behind a series of actions, leading to a change and a healing that makes for our greater happiness and peace. It is the motivation we long for, and it is given to us so that we can begin to lead a life of greater wholeness. Conversion occurs through wanting it and then allowing the slow process of desire to become translated into actions.

The Spirit calls us, and offers us his gifts. We are invited, never forced, to respond to them. If we do, a happier, freer, more serene future is ours.

Conclusion

In this chapter I have tried to relate various experiences that illustrate the consequences of surrendering to the Holy Spirit. His gifts are ours if we ask for them, and as we have seen in the various episodes I described the asking is not always done in formal prayer, nor are the moments of spiritual direction limited to retreats or even to ongoing spiritual direction. The Spirit, fortunately for us, is around at all times, eager to shower us with good things, longing to fill us with the peace and happiness that he alone can bring. The filling up, of course, calls first for the emptying out, but once we say "yes" to the process, it is made meaningful. No matter how great the pain of being emptied, if we know why, we can endure it. We can endure being drained of all our self-indulgences so that we can be filled with the Spirit, and in him have all that is good given to us, "a full measure, pressed down, shaken together, and running over" (Lk. 6:38).

Chapter Three
WHAT TO LOOK FOR
IN A SPIRITUAL DIRECTOR

Introduction

Having related various instances of the Holy Spirit at work in his people, we now have to investigate how one can go about receiving the spiritual direction that so often has facilitated the gifts of the Spirit in people's lives. In order to do this I think it is necessary to try to understand what sort of a person can be a spiritual director. This is, it seems to me, a necessary task to undertake, for many misconceptions exist as to who a spiritual director might be. If we can clear up these ambiguities we may recognize with a greater ease who is a director and who ought to think about becoming one. For spiritual direction is a gift given to many more people than are currently engaged in it. Perhaps if one can realize that the gift is not restricted to religious or priests, then one may begin to see potential directors in one's own "secular" midst, perhaps even within the generous stirrings of compassion and love in one's own heart.

Spiritual directors are sinners who through many failures are conscious of their own need for God. They are familiar with the workings of his ways and steep themselves daily in a humble listening to the Lord in their minds and hearts. They know of their own vulnerability and seek always to learn through various sources how to help people get closer to God; they are humble students never quite satisfied that they have all or even some of the answers as they listen, as attentively as they can, to another's account of prayer.

But directors are confident in God's competence in helping others to come to him, and, knowing this, they feel competent in their own incompetence.

A person seeking spiritual direction needs to be aware of this. The director is not one who is better than the person being directed, but rather is a fellow pilgrim who wants to help others to know God in their lives. Any sincere Christian can become a good spiritual director. Many directees then can be potential directors, for have not all sincere Christians experienced their sinfulness and known the Father's forgiving love?

I believe this is a most important point. Many lay persons have expressed frustration to me regarding their inability to find a spiritual director, and many others have complained that, having found a director, that person—as sincere as he or she may be—was not able to respond to and consequently guide the directee in the life of the Spirit. It is a legitimate frustration that deserves a serious answer.

It seems to me that we are living more and more in a post-clerical Church. There are increasingly less priests and religious to go around, and those that are around are so busy that it would be most unfair to expect them to take on the additional responsibility, to say nothing of the time and energy, to become competent spiritual directors. And this is not necessarily a bad thing for our purposes, for the dearth of clergy is causing an increasing awareness among the laity to assume a greater responsibility in the Church we all belong to. There is no reason why the non-clerical members of our Church—the lay men and women who after all comprise well over ninety-five percent of the Church—cannot become good spiritual directors. In fact, an increasing number of Christians are recognizing this and are beginning to do something about it through various programs and workshops designed to train spiritual directors. And there are quite a few of them available. Christian periodicals frequently advertise such programs, as well as retreat opportunities, for all categories of people. It is rare for any of these programs to discriminate in favor of priests and religious only. Indeed the trend ought to be moving counter to that, for the Church of the twenty-first century needs competent and well-trained non-clerical spiritual leaders working with the clergy as "co-heirs with Christ" for its work to truly take on the universal dimensions that the kingdom of

God on earth calls us to assume.

Hence a potential directee may also be a potential director and may wish to seek out information on how to become one, inquiring at the parish or chancery or a local retreat house or community of men or women religious. If none of these places can offer any significant information one can always contact a national organization such as Retreats International for assistance. This new service has published directories of directed retreat centers in the United States and Canada, as well as a fairly comprehensive listing of 482 directors' names together with personal backgrounds on each one. These directories can be obtained by writing directly to Retreats International, 1112 Memorial Library, Notre Dame, Indiana 46556.

A factor of considerable importance that may enter in here arises out of a prejudice that should definitely be buried. Spiritual directors do not have to be men. Some of the greatest spiritual directors the world has known—St. Teresa of Avila, for example—have been women. Today many a fine spiritual director is a woman, and consequently a resource for finding a competent director could very well be at one's own doorstep in a local residence of religious women. Of course here too, as with priests and men religious, the dearth of women religious today makes it difficult for one seeking direction to locate a competent directress, but then again one may very well receive directions from the local convent as to where to find one. Perhaps all that a person needs to do is ask in the right places.

Further—and this is another prejudice whose demise needs to be hastened—a spiritual director does not have to be a Catholic. Christians of other denominations who are prayerful people most certainly can be competent directors.

But who is a competent spiritual director? What is it that enables a person to enable the spirit in another to bloom? Here I will try to answer that question in some detail, hoping that in the process the potential directee will find a profile of his or her future director. Perhaps you also can find that within yourself the ingredients for a spiritual director are already present. In that case the potential directee may very well be the spiritual director of the future and could be receiving an invitation from the Spirit of truth to look deeper into oneself and find there a call waiting to be discovered that can bring abundant life to many. But what should one look for? I hope to answer that question under five headings.

First, a spiritual director deals with spiritual things in another. Hence it is legitimate to expect that a director be closely in touch with the spiritual aspects of his or her own life as well. This means that a director must be a person of prayer, open to the Spirit in one's own heart and open to another director on an ongoing basis. A good director is one who is first a docile directee open to another's guidance and help.

Further, one may also legitimately expect a director to have a gift for discerning between the good and the evil movements within a person. Most often it is in this discernment that God's will is to be found.

As a third ingredient one may also expect a director to be a good listener. While these qualifications reflect more on talents that have to be developed rather than skills that have to be acquired, there is also a certain amount of training that a director should have as one seeking to enable the gifts of the Spirit in another. I will try to outline a training program for the potential director and discuss it as my fourth heading. Finally, and certainly of key importance, the director needs to be aware that as a director one is in partnership with God who is the true guide. I call this awareness being a competent incompetent. I think we have to do our part, but I also think that we have to be deeply and sincerely convinced that it is truly the Lord who effects changes in people's hearts and minds and not we who do so.

Often this fact can become obfuscated within us; then, rather than being enablers we could become detractors of God's Spirit. However the reality of spiritual direction tends to keep one humble and aware of who is truly changing people's hearts.

But no matter how much we may be aware of this it is possible to forget it, especially when one is involved in a particularly difficult situation. Spiritual direction is not always smooth sailing. I will try to deal with this in a realistic way as I elaborate on the qualifications the potential director ought to have.

In the previous chapter I offered several examples of the role that spiritual directors play in a person's life. Often the accounts I related left out the many struggles and disappointments inherent for directors engaged in helping others find wholeness. This was because I was trying to heighten the actions of the Spirit in a person's life so as to offer a clearer understanding of what the Spirit brings. But the world of the spirits is a world of ambiguity and uncertainty, and potential directors need to be aware that occasionally they may find themselves confronted not with a healing but with confusion and a sense of helplessness. Often the one directing has to admit to a directee that the way to proceed is uncertain and quite unclear. And on occasion the director has to ask the directee to go to another for help, admitting the inability or helplessness to be of service. But as long as one keeps in mind the point of it all—God's glory rendered visible in a human being fully alive—then the personal failures become somehow intertwined in the redemptive mystery itself, and they make us enter ever more humbly into the glory of an Easter Sunday that will always be waiting around the next corner.

A Person of Prayer

Spiritual directors ought to be people who pray a lot. They know through many hours of silent listening and considerable struggle the richness of God's forgiveness in their lives. When we come to directors for guidance, therefore, we come to companions who have often been hurt and bewildered, uncertain of their own progress, but who nevertheless have experienced over and over again the firm and gentle hand of a loving God leading them forward toward a wholeness and a holiness that all of us yearn for.

One who prays is one who has repeatedly walked with hope in darkness. The vulnerability Jesus experienced in the garden of Gethsemane on that night of pain is what the person of prayer is called to live—just as the glory of Easter Sunday is the end we are called to proclaim through the confidence of faith. One who has not endured the night can hardly empathize truthfully with another who, while sweating blood, is crying to a silent God for help and salvation. The director needs to be a person who has experienced failure. And more than that, a director needs to be one who has been aware of being lifted up from that failure by God.

A director's awareness of the process of redemption in one's own life occurs in prayer. It is out of this awareness that a director can cooperate with God in bringing alive the promise of the resurrection to a directee who may be sorely wounded. For one wondering about becoming a spiritual director, this awareness of the redemptive mystery in one's own life, no matter how specifically it has been experienced, is a key prerequisite.

Prayer is the vehicle through which God communicates his love for his people. It is the contact point with God through which we discipline ourselves to listen regularly in our hearts to that which is most true, most loving, most God-like within us. In prayer we live out a love relationship with a God who is constantly making overtures to our hearts, longing for that day when we finally fall into his arms where all will be taken up forever. Potential directors ought to be people in close personal touch with this Lord of unashamed love. They ought to be people who see regular contact with God as essential to their well-being and treat prayer as a vital and indeed intrinsic part of their lives. Prayer becomes not "something that I have to get in" but my way of living.

There are various ways a Christian can become a person of prayer. But all of them presume a willingness to want it and to work hard at it over one's lifetime. Yet whatever the methods used—meditation, contemplation, and so on—the regular discipline of setting time aside for this purpose alone is indispensable. Of a spiritual director one has a right to expect this.

Further, since there are so many methods of prayer, and since their use depends on the movements of the Spirit and not on any pre-arranged plan, an ideal director can be legitimately expected to know most if not all of them through personal experience and have the flexibility to use one or the other as the need arises. Methods of prayer are ways that have evolved over the years as vehicles through which contact with God has become possible. They are the fruits of centuries of praying, and they are available to us as a part of the rich heritage of being a people set apart by a God of love. None of them is to be upheld as inherently better than another, but rather all are options, to be used or set aside at various times, depending primarily on the inner movements within that individual at prayer time. Let me give you an example.

A retreatant once started his retreat by telling me that he had no particular request of God for this retreat; he just possessed a quiet desire to get closer to him. Listening to him I thought that I perceived a simplicity and a genuineness, and I felt that the Lord was inviting him to concentrate on Psalm 131, dealing with child-like trust in God. I could as well have given him some other passage on simplicity, but this one came to mind as he talked. Listening to the harmony within me, I offered it to him as a suggestion. I was not sure, but when he eagerly accepted it he confirmed for me that the Holy Spirit had indeed guided me to that particular psalm for him. However, it is important to know of several passages on any given topic for prayer, for if, for instance, he had not accepted it, I needed some other alternatives to fall back on. Why should one passage be acceptable and another not, especially if they are on the same subject? The word of God is alive, and a small nuance, even one word, present in one and missing in another could make the difference in hearing or not hearing God's particular message in that prayer. Hence the director, alert to his own feelings and to the feelings of the directee, suggests a Scripture passage or some other prayer and, with the collaborative acceptance of that prayer by the directee, offers it as the vehicle for making God's voice audible at that given moment. If there is uncertainty or uneasiness in accepting it, then further discernment is called for, on both their parts.

A person of prayer is a loving person. Anyone who allows the Spirit to become intimate is permitting Love itself entrance. That persons's actions are then motivated by love, and one can legitimately expect a director to be a kind, caring, loving person. And being kind and loving must not conjure up "meek and mild," for a director who is kind and truthfully loving must be able to confront a person with boldness at times so that the Spirit of truth can be better evoked. Spiritual direction deals with affairs of the heart, intimate encounters between God and his people, and hence there is little room for ungracious behavior in those seeking to give help. A director who loves much can be detected easily as one who prays much.

I remember a day not long ago during a seminar on spiritual direction when the instructor was discussing prayer with a group of potential directors. He pointed out that as directors we need to be caring people but not phonies who "put on masks of concern" for the benefit of the directee but afterward ridicule the person in one's own mind or to another. There is no room for this sort of thing in the spiritual life, for it indicates a person not in touch with personal failure and sin, and perhaps more importantly not in touch with a God who forgives repeatedly and still remains respectful of our "space," as the contemporary idiom puts it. Reverence for others, especially those who entrust their deepest selves to another, rises primarily from the personal experience of having been accepted and respected by God. And these experiences are intimate ones taking place in the depths of one's heart when, after a particular incident that had failure written all over it, one goes to one's Abba, Father, and finds solace in a gentle and forgiving hand. This happens when one prays. A director must let this happen regularly, for through it one discovers the meaning of love and hears again the words of Jesus in a wonderfully personal way: "There is no need to be afraid, little flock, for it has pleased your Father to give you the kingdom" (Lk. 12:32).

The Gift of Discernment

Spiritual direction is a gift, as St. Paul, in his First Letter to the Corinthians, clearly states. There are many gifts, he says, and he goes on to list some of them, including the gift of recognizing spirits.

There is a variety of gifts but always the same Spirit. . . . One may have the gift of preaching with wisdom given him by the Spirit . . . another the gift of recognizing spirits. . . . All these are the work of one and the same Spirit, who distributes different gifts to different people just as he chooses (1 Cor. 12:4-11).

Spiritual direction cannot be something that ordination or religious vows can prepare us for. That would be like expecting a general practitioner in medicine to perform delicate neurosurgery just because he is a doctor. Neurosurgery requires far more training than a non-specialized school in medicine can provide and a talent for the work that, in the final analysis, no amount of training can supply. So also with spiritual direction. A potential director may get the training in all sincerity but not be a very good discerner of spirits. This is because discerning the spirits is a talent that needs to be developed. I want to reemphasize here that ordination or religious vows do not necessarily guarantee competence in spiritual direction. Many a non-clerical Christian could do far better if endowed with this talent than a priest or religious. It is up to the individual to determine whether one has this talent freed from the prejudice of feeling unworthy simply because one belongs to the laity.

The ability to discern spirits is both gift and training, and the training should ideally elicit the gift that lies unrecognized. But how is one to know if one has this gift? Perhaps a partial way of determining this is to discern with a spiritual director how well one does with oneself. If one can accurately discern and identify the various movements and spirits going on within oneself, then maybe one has the potential to do that for someone else. But what are these spirits, and what makes some good and some bad? St. Ignatius of Loyola in his *Spiritual Exercises* tells us that they are "the different movements produced in the soul" and proceeds to give us rules "for recognizing those that are good, to admit them, and those that are bad, to reject them" (*Spiritual Exercises,* annotation #313). They are the various feelings that emanate from within us, motivating us to some actions that are either good or bad. They can also originate from without us, from other people in relation with us or from powers that are beyond our human abilities to grasp. While they are felt movements, they engage the mind in various places, and both the mind and feelings, in partnership, produce the actions that result. But—and underlining the complexity of the spiritual world —it is also possible for the feelings to evolve independently of the mind. And of course the mind can often educe a feeling. It is the task of the spiritual director to decipher all of this and guide a person, conscious that it is being done in partnership with that person and with God. Consequently the movements occurring in the directee are understood, and the right course of action that will lead that person to a happier, more peace-filled state can be realized.

St. Ignatius proceeds to give us some of the symptoms to watch out for in discerning the spirits. He observes in annotation #315 of the *Spiritual Exercises* that "it is characteristic of the evil spirit to harass with anxiety, to afflict with sadness, to raise obstacles backed by fallacious reasonings that disturb the soul." Also, he goes on to say that evil spirits can be detected when there is "darkness of soul, turmoil of spirit, inclination to what is low and earthly, restlessness rising from many disturbances and temptations which lead to want of faith, want of hope, want of love."

Likewise he tells us the symptoms to watch out for when a person is experiencing the interior movements caused by the good spirits. He says: "It is characteristic of the good spirit . . . to give courage and strength, consolations, tears, inspirations and peace" (annotation #315). The gift of tears that he mentions is described by him as "when one sheds tears that move to the love of God, whether it be because of sorrow for sins, or because of the sufferings of Christ our Lord, or for any other reason that is immediately directed to the praise and service of God. . . . I call consolation every increase of faith, hope, and love, and all interior joy that invites and attracts to what is heavenly and to the salvation of one's soul by filling it with peace and quiet in its Creator and Lord" (annotation #316).

It is the task of spiritual directors to discern these interior movements within a person. They ought to be trusting in grace, confident that the Holy Spirit is present within the directees and within themselves, and in the dynamic of the interchange between them as well. Then they can listen to the spirits and, discerning the good from the bad, suggest to the directee a suitable course of action.

These movements occur in prayer, but also at various other times. The spirit world is a quite active one, and there are many opportunities for the good or the bad spirits to achieve an ascendancy in our lives. Often the director experiences vulnerability while discerning spirits with another. And often the fact that direction is a three-way contract becomes sharpened into a pronounced focus. It is always good to remember that a director is as susceptible to the spirits as the directee, and when one seeks to help another to be freed of something, the sense of one's own insecurities and fears can be easily augmented. It is essential to remember that God is the real director, and that both director and directee are sinners seeking to realize God's actions through their conversations.

I remember an experience of this three-way partnership in discernment that I once had; hopefully it may help explicate what I am trying to explain.

When she first walked into my office she appeared cold and reserved. I had never met her before and recall feeling some slight nervousness, for she had a somewhat haughty demeanor that I found intimidating. I invited her to sit down, and after sharing a few pleasantries I asked her to tell me a little bit about herself.

She had been a faithful Catholic during her childhood and was brought up believing in a God who was powerful, demanding and swift in exacting retribution for transgressions against the laws of his Church. She thought of these laws as endless lists of "Thou shalts" and "Thou shalt nots." For several years, operating out of these fears, she persevered in practicing her religion, but not with any great conviction. Then she fell in love with a man not of her faith, and against the wishes of her family she married him. She was fearful of God's punishment for doing so but felt convinced that this was what she had to do. Less than two years after their marriage, however, her husband was killed in an accident and the bottom fell out of whatever faith she had. She believed that her husband's death was a direct act of God's retributive justice. Guilt, anger and depression consumed her for years thereafter. Thoughts of suicide were constantly on her mind, and it was only a lack of courage that prevented her from carrying them out into action. Then, almost as a blessing in disguise, she found out that she had developed cancer. She chose to do nothing about it, accepting the disease defiantly, as if to tell God. "I can take whatever you choose to inflict on me."

As time went on and the cancer progressed at a slow, steady pace, fear took over from her defiance, and she decided that maybe she was wrong about God. But the search for God that she embarked on proved fruitless. Wanting to make sure before finally giving up she had come to make this retreat, and so here she was.

I was taken up by her moving account and realized that as I had listened to her my feelings of fear about her had dissipated, to be replaced by compassion. I found that her apparent haughtiness was a mask. She, too, had been grappling with fear when she first entered. I proceeded to reassure her, saying that all God expected from her right then was honesty with herself and with me. She listened, but then protested, arguing that her first concern was not what God expected but whether there was a God at all.

Again I felt threatened. I felt fear and a sense of incompetence. How could I prove God's existence to her? How could I convince her in a few minutes that God does indeed exist? As she kept insisting on proof for his existence, however, I struggled to respond to her and recall praying at the same time to God, asking him for help. The evil movements within me started to dissipate even as I talked to her. I told her that in the final analysis I couldn't prove God's existence to her or anyone else, that it was a matter of faith, and that we could perhaps do better not to try to prove his existence right then but to accept it as a given, and proceed from there. I wasn't sure what I was saying but felt within me that this was the evil spirit at work, seeking to confound the issue by a lot of intellectual haranguing. Discerning this movement I proposed that she set aside the question for now and simply accept the fact that she was here and that it would be good to give herself to the experience of the retreat on faith.

The next three days were routine. She agreed to go along with my direction. She reflected on some Old Testament Scripture passages and enjoyed the trees and the flowers, but essentially she felt that she was just marking time. She described her prayer as shallow and unconsoling, and each day she came in to see me wringing her hands with frustration and almost boasting of her failure. "Nothing is happening. See—I told you so," was the unspoken point she was making.

I kept asking her what she was feeling, for I was discerning someone who had used her intellect to shut out her feelings. I felt that if the Spirit could unlock her feelings, all her arguments against God's existence—she persisted in bringing this up—could become secondary. Meanwhile, I had been praying for her, asking God to visit her with some sense of his love, especially his forgiving love. I felt confident that he was with me, and that I needed to be patient, trusting in his ways and his time, not mine or hers.

On the fourth day God showed himself to her. She told me about it during our conference: "The day dawned for me as every other day had," she began. "I was sure it would be filled with tears and frustration, but it was not to be so. In a quiet moment of meditation the breakthrough came. Suddenly, and for no logical reason, I knew there was a God. The initial sense of delight and achievement was quickly followed by great sadness and sorrow. I had neglected this kind and loving God all of my life. I had missed the joy of knowing him for so many years." She was subdued as she recounted her grace to me but within me I felt a combination of relief, gratitude and deep joy. I felt that these signs of the Holy Spirit in me affirmed her in her prayer, and I suggested that she remain in her present state of consolation for the next day relishing the gift God had given her.

The rest of the retreat was hard. Her breakthrough was just the beginning, and she was filled with sorrow and shame for her past life. But I felt at peace with this, for in discerning the various spirits at work I felt that her anguish was coming from a genuine sense of repentance and was quite different from the anguish of despair with which she entered the retreat.

She ended her retreat peacefully, and though aware that she had only just begun, she was eager to "get on with it" so that God's love could finally find a home within her.

The remaining months of her life consisted of prayer, study and continuing doubts about her religion. No, her questions were not all answered, but as she told me some months later, "I will continue to seek the answers, but the answers are no longer of paramount importance, for I now believe that there is a loving God who accepts me."

She looked at me with an air of confidence and nodded. I smiled at her, feeling within myself the peace that continued to affirm the Spirit of truth at work in her.

She died a few months later. Some of the last words she spoke to me were words of hope. She said, "I know God will not take away all of today's fears nor tomorrow's pain. But I believe that if I continue to bring my problems and my suffering to him, he will give me the strength to live each day. He will give me inner peace. Why do I believe this? I believe because I have found faith."

Discerning the spirits with faith calls one to be a part of the action. The director is in partnership with the directee, and both are in partnership with God who points first one, then the other, in the direction of life. Discerning the various movements of God within oneself is a subtle process, but once engaged upon, it guarantees for us who believe the helping hand of God.

But discernment is not just an individual process. If anything the spiritual life ought to lead us out to others in a greater love and a more gracious patience. Furthermore, one cannot always discern accurately without help. Often one may need a group discernment before determining in what direction to guide the directee. And this calls for making oneself vulnerable before the directee, admitting uncertainty and helplessness, and likewise admitting that at times one needs help in discerning the spirits from others. Of course, this always presumes a strict collective confidentiality, with the anonymity of the directee an understood presupposition. In fact if anonymity cannot be maintained no group discernment ought to be attempted. In this case, though, one could take aside one director from the team and privately ask for help. If prudent it would be good to first secure the directee's permission.

Let me tell you of a retreat experience I once had. It will help to delineate the vulnerability to which a director is susceptible, as well as the importance of discerning the spirits with accuracy, even though that may call for a group discernment.

She was tall, with a pleasant face that reflected openness as well as grief. Her eyes appeared troubled. Our first meeting was cordial and kept on a fairly superficial plane while we both got to know one another. I asked her, after a while, to talk to me about her prayer.

Without too much difficulty she opened up and talked at some length about it. I got the impression of a quite prayerful woman, one who was dedicated to leading a life of faith and who didn't appear to have any motive in this retreat greater than advancing in her relationship with the Lord. I decided at this initial meeting not to probe, allowing the questions I had about her apparent disquiet to wait for a later meeting. I was not even sure whether they were, in fact, signs of restlessness. I suggested that she begin slowing down, setting aside any anxieties or trepidations she might have at this early stage of the retreat by going for a relaxing walk with nature, allowing the beauties there to bring a tranquility and peace to her soul. I told her to pray the prayer of all things and described it briefly.

Invariably a retreatant enters a retreat exhausted, tense, and scattered in mind and heart. I find it often helpful, consequently, to allow the person to ease into the atmosphere of prayer and recollection by suggesting the prayer of all things. I ask that the person take the day wondering at the things of nature, relishing their beauty and avoiding any tendencies to formulate prayers of gratitude to God or the like. I urge that one absorb the beauty of a flower, for example, and allow the feelings so evoked to remain undisturbed by any intrusions of the intellect. Perhaps the best description of the prayer of all things is Hopkins' idea of "inscape" which is "our ability to perceive a unified complex of sensible qualities that are unique to and most typical of any given thing." And this perception is not in any philosophical or intellectual sense, but a fact that speaks of the grandeur of God, so that as one perceives and is absorbed into the magnificence of a tree, the feelings of beauty so aroused offer a glimpse of the beauty of God and also help attune oneself to one's feelings in general. In a retreat experience, where feelings in prayer are so significant, any fine tuning of one's feelings cannot help but be of service.

The next day we started off with her recalling to me the various moods and feelings of the previous day and the occasional thoughts that accompanied them. I picked up a genuineness in her that I liked—a willingness to be open about her prayer life and a desire to truly deepen her love for the Lord.

After listening to her, I started wondering whether the initial impression of some trouble within was my misinterpretation based on a simple nervousness at the start of the retreat. At any rate she was not providing me with any data to that effect that I could pursue at the moment, so there was no opening to ask any further questions. I simply suggested some Scripture passages on God's love and left it at that.

When I say "I had no opening" I mean that her accounting of her feelings in prayer the day before did not correspond to the feeling of trouble that I was experiencing within me, so I had no excuse to ask her about it; it could very well be just my subjective feeling with no basis in reality. On the other hand feelings like this, intuitions if you will, are to be listened to and not ignored. Often it is through them that the Spirit is speaking to the director, and it is the director's task to be able to detect those movements.

Frequently this is quite difficult to do, for the movements of the spirits can be so subtle that they may escape detection for a long time. It calls for an alertness to signs and a humble awareness that many a time, no matter how alert one may be, hints are missed and perhaps an opportunity for a grace is passed over.

Over the next five days—it was an eight-day retreat—she experienced feelings of peace and contentment in the knowledge that she was loved as she was and not for anything she did. She was in a general state of happiness. In prayer she would frequently break out spontaneously into songs of praise to God. These are some of the signs of the good Spirit, and as long as there were movements of peace and joy taking place I was content to guide her in the direction of God's love, the direction suggested by the peaceful mood she was in when reflecting on this subject.

The next three days were similar in movement. I continued listening but failed to detect anything unusual. She was doing well with her periods of prayer, not encountering any difficulty with the full hours of prayer. In fact she was looking forward to them. I had suggested that she increase the frequency of her prayer periods, and she eagerly acquiesced, now praying four to five hours a day.

Sensing that she was sufficiently steeped in the experience of God's love for her, I suggested that we move on to meditating on God's forgiving love of our sins and how he always forgives them if we but ask him. I asked her how she felt about moving into these meditations, and she responded affirmatively.

The retreat was in the fifth day and it was going well. There were no indications of being closed on her part. I felt that if her meditations on sin would continue to trigger peace and consolation I could just about put my initial concerns to rest. I suggested that she remember the most significant failures of her life and then beg God to forgive them. I urged her not to go from one sin to the next until she felt his forgiving love for that particular sin first. She complied and was almost eager to do it. I repeated the emphasis for the meditations—that they should be centered on his forgiveness of her sins and not on the sins themselves.

The next day I waited for her with some disquietude, wondering how her prayers had gone. I think that as much as one believes, and in fact knows quite well, that the Holy Spirit is the real director, one feels a sense of responsibility toward a directee. It calls for a constant alacrity toward one's own needs to "play God" and to allow the valid and not the less valid sense of responsibility—read "overprotectiveness"—to creep in. When she came in, she exuded peace and a true air of freedom. I felt harmony as she recounted the various feelings she had experienced the previous day. She had immersed herself generously in remembering her sins and felt deeply the ensuing forgiveness of them.

My feeling of harmony reflected a sense of peace inside me that her prayer was a genuine experience of being loved by God, and that this love was felt in a tangible way that evoked a state of well-being.

Content that all was going well, I asked her whether she would like, at this point, to reflect on the way God went about forgiving us. I asked her whether she would feel good about praying on the passion of our Lord.

Almost instantaneously her face changed, registering alarm and fear. I asked her what the matter was. All we were going to do was meditate on the greatest act of love, the greatest proof of God's love for us. Wondering whether it was the sufferings of the passion that she feared, I assured her that we need touch on them only as the context of God's love for us—that it was his love that we would pray on.

She wasn't listening. I saw her begin to tremble visibly and witnessed her face contort with fear and anxiety. At this point I knew that a discordant note had definitely been struck and felt obligated to pursue it. I asked her what was wrong. She shook her head silently. I coaxed, assuring her of my support and care for her. I promised her that I would do my best to help whatever it was. Her only answer was silence. I kept talking gently and soothingly, urging her to talk to me and saying that it probably was not as bad as she felt it was.

Symptoms of the evil spirit were evident, and I knew something was wrong. Often, however, these symptoms are not as evident and the director's astuteness at discerning their presence becomes that much harder. In this retreat what now happened is very curious and bears retelling. It illustrates well how a director can become helpless and personally quite vulnerable when directing another. I think it also underlines the importance of the discernment of spirits, not just by the director with a directee but between directors as well.

Finally she did talk—slowly, falteringly. It appears that for years the cross was a focal image of evil for her. The image of a crucifix would send her into fearful moods of depression and anxiety. It made her very restless, filling her with deep fears and horrible fantasies. She saw the devil laughing at her from the cross. The body of Christ crucified was the devil triumphant. I think this is an instance where knowledge of some psychology could have proved invaluable. While I was vaguely aware of the various psychological implications of what she was saying, I did not know enough to be able to help.

Hence I didn't attempt to understand it. I just listened. She talked without faltering now. In fact, it came out in a flood of words. In my office, there was a crucifix facing me that was on the wall directly behind her. While listening to her, I had glanced at that crucifix a few times. Now, I glanced at it again.

I turned cold. I felt fear within me, and deep anxieties started to develop. The more I looked at the crucifix, the more fearful I became. Therefore I forced myself to concentrate on her words and not look at it while she was in the room.

I urged her to concentrate on God's love, pointed out that it was crucial to stick to her meditations on the passion as I had outlined them, and then spoke to her of the evil spirit. I showed her the aberration he was trying to work on her—to take the image of his love for us and distort it so that it appeared an object of fear. She looked at me, but I don't think she was hearing me.

After she left, I looked at the crucifix again. Again I began feeling terrible fears, and I felt my body turn cold with fright. Amazed, I noticed myself literally trembling. Then I started to have fantasies—horrible fantasies of the devil on the cross, mocking, laughing, scolding.

I left the room and went in search of my fellow directors. I felt that I was losing my mind. After a while I found them, and we talked. I outlined to them what had happened and asked them whether this was my imagination running riot. The value of working on a team flitted through my mind with gratitude. I sensed that I needed them, not only to ask them to discern with me what was going on with the retreatant but also to help me discern what was happening within me. I felt that I was losing my grip on reality and consequently felt that I was at the time quite unable to discern for another. My co-directors took me seriously. One of them had had two or three similar experiences; the other pointed out to me that what I was experiencing was very much what exorcists experience. However, they were not sure how to proceed. We decided to pray. Afterward one of them suggested that it might be a good idea if all three of us went into the chapel together and pray before the crucifix there. The other director, however, disagreed. It was his opinion that it was quite essential for me to go before the crucifix in the chapel, but that I should go alone.

In the small chapel was a life-size crucifix with corpus dominating the room. Its existence had crossed my mind, and while looking for the other directors I had gone up to the chapel only to find myself unable to enter because of what was on the other side of the doors. I now felt great fear, yet trusted that going there was the right thing to do.

All day long I tried to go into the chapel but could not. The fears continued, and I grew extremely restless. At liturgy that evening—which mercifully was held in a room other than the chapel—it was all I could do to sit still. I noticed my retreatant having a similar problem.

That night was a nightmare. I couldn't sleep. I was tormented by all manner of evil thoughts and fantasies, seeing imaginary lights moving around my room at one point. I longed for daylight. Finally, it arrived.

I got up, prayed briefly, and decided that in order to overcome this, I first needed to be in the state of grace. Therefore I went in search of one of the directors, who was also a personal friend, and received the sacrament of reconciliation. Then, not feeling too much better, I knew I had to go to the chapel.

It was hard, but finally I opened the door, slid in, and sat in a corner chair, my eyes transfixed on the monstrous gibbet. I remained there, almost unable to move, panicky and filled with genuine terror. Then I noticed, out of the corner of my eye, that the

Blessed Sacrament was there in a little tabernacle on the side. Making a titanic effort, I took a quick look at it. I kept telling myself that in a special way the real living God was alive in the chapel. There was nothing alive on that cross. Slowly, over a fairly short/long period of time—I don't know how long—the momentary glances at the tabernacle became longer, until finally I started realizing that peace was present when I looked at the tabernacle, as opposed to fear and restlessness when I looked at the cross. Slowly I surrendered to the peace by fixing my gaze on the dwelling of the living God, not on the image of the cross. Correspondingly, the peace deepened, and eventually took hold of me again.

Remembering this event now, I recall how helpless I really was. The director was as vulnerable and as powerless as his directee. It is a very humbling state to be in but it seems to me that it could often be the very vehicle through which the Holy Spirit can regain entrance.

After my ordeal I walked out of that chapel deeply confident in God's power. I went up to my ofice to await my retreatant who was due to see me shortly. When she walked in she was smiling and evinced a calmness that was quite remarkable considering the state she had been in so recently. After inviting her to be seated I asked her how her prayer had gone. "It's gone," she said. "The fear of the cross has gone. I feel a surprising peace inside and a sense of confidence that the fear has gone for good." I smiled, encouraging her to go on. "It was a hellish struggle," she continued. "My meditations were filled with distractions and all kinds of weird images and sick ideas. But I struggled through them all. Then this morning I was meditating on the crucifixion itself and slowly Jesus looked directly at me from the cross, and I saw a gentle, saddened look in his eyes. And he whispered my name. I felt peace begin to enter at that time, and for the rest of that prayer it deepened. I know I am not afraid of the cross anymore. I feel that a power has been broken." After her retreat I shared with her the struggle I had endured and how the Holy Spirit had regained entrance into my soul just before our conference. "It's a funny coincidence," she said. "That was about the time I was making my meditation on the crucifixion."

The vulnerability and weakness we both shared had been the

vehicle for a change for the better within us. I know that the movements of the spirits were quite strong and not typical of a person's prayer, but they left a lasting impression on both of us and serve to illustrate the necessity of being able to differentiate between the good and evil movements so that one can determine what course of action needs to be taken. In this instance my co-directors' discernment of the spirits and their consequent suggestions set the proper course of events rolling so that the Holy Spirit could eventually regain entrance into our lives. And this points up the importance of directing with others, or at least having another available and willing to help when one is directing.

The subtleties of the spirit world, the fearful consequences as well as the glorious freedoms possible in it, are hopefully described in this experience. For those seeking to direct others in it, the gift of discernment enables them to walk boldly with another into realms that are not the common walks of humankind. It is important to enter it prepared and to be open, always open to asking for help from others who can, as in this instance, give just the right suggestion to make the difference.

A Good Listener

The world of the spirits, as different as it is from the material world around us, calls for a far greater alertness for its revelation to become evident in our lives. From a world of noise and turbulence, we need to become people attuned to the sound of falling snowflakes when we enter this world of the spirits. It calls for attentive listening.

Listening to anyone takes effort, and the more one *chooses* to become attentive the more one does. Occasionally I find myself allowing my concentration to drift, finding that the person's conversation is not really affecting me on any significant level. I hear the words being spoken and put on a mask of attentiveness, but I am thinking of something else. A spiritual director is called to make a special effort to prevent this from happening. When someone is speaking of one's life, the director owes it to that person to be as alert and attentive as possible, not just out of a sense of obligation or duty but rather from genuine concern.

However if one is finding it genuinely difficult to listen to another's account it could also be a signal that that person is being superficial and is not dipping significantly into his or her life. The difficulty in paying attention could be merely an indication that there is nothing worthwhile being said to pay attention to. It could be a signal that one needs to ask questions to lead the directees into a deeper and more honest appraisal of themselves and their lives in the Spirit.

In order to listen with full attention, one must choose to love the person first. This is something that both directors and directees presume is the case, but quite often it is a false presumption. Often it is hard to love someone, and it takes effort to do so. But the directors who do not even try or who hide behind a facade of "professionalism" are really being dishonest with the directee and with themselves as well. The professionalism required of the Christian is the command of Jesus to "love one another as I have loved you" (Jn. 15:12), and the whole point of direction is to help someone arrive at this love in a lifelong process of realization. With the Spirit of Jesus we choose to love the other; without it the choice does not exist.

I recall once a co-director telling me of his firm belief that this was just a job and that I should not allow any personal involvement with the retreatant to occur. And he was quite right. To become emotionally involved with the retreatant would make me become ineffectual, but that must not become an excuse to hold oneself aloof from the directee. It operates out of the command of Jesus, to love and be loved, as he loved us. It is also never just a job, for to the extent that it is considered that way, love is made "just a job."

Let me try to explain what sort of listening I am talking about. When listening to a person in direction—I must differentiate this type of listening from the polite attentiveness to another at a social gathering—the director is engaged in listening to two movements. First, one listens to the words being spoken, taking in the factual data that the person is relating even while listening to the feelings expressed non-verbally. Then one listens to the feelings evoked within oneself by both. So, for instance, when a retreatant is describing a prayer experience, I allow myself to become a part of that experience in the listening, and I begin to respond to the movements being described through my own feelings. If the accounting is a peace-filled, happy description of God's love I listen to myself and see whether these same feelings are being evoked in me. If so, I am at harmony with the retreatant's account and recognize the good Spirit at work; if not, I then probe further, asking questions and seeking clarifications to ferret out the truth. It might be that the evil spirit is at work but merely presenting itself to the pray-er as a Spirit of consolation and love. This is disharmony. It calls for a keen listening to oneself, and since often the feelings evoked in oneself are ambiguous, it calls for faith as well—faith in the Spirit of truth.

For the Spirit is in the midst of this listening process, and he is found uniquely in this dynamic interplay of listening both to the other and to oneself. The director is called upon to recognize that and to humbly respond to the Spirit by responding to the directee from the heart and not from the head alone.

Once I was listening to a retreatant describe his experience in prayer. It was on God's forgiving love. He had given himself fully to the prayer. He had made the meditation faithfully during the full hour we had agreed upon, and nothing happened. He just sat there, bored and quite dry. He was restless, glanced at his watch frequently, and just couldn't get into it. While I was listening, I started feeling an uneasiness within myself. It wasn't that his account was unusual or that he failed to give me sufficient data; I just started feeling that there was something more here than just another dry prayer period. I asked him to go over his description again and continued to listen to my own feelings. He repeated much the same account, but in his repetition I started deriving the clarity I needed about my feeling of uneasiness. And that provided me with the insight to ask the right question: "Is there a sin in your life that you feel God has not forgiven you for?" I asked. That did it. With a sudden obvious change of mood he told me there was, and he went on to tell me about it. If, on the other hand, another retreatant had come in and described his prayer using identical words, it could be possible that in listening to myself I would have found nothing of disharmony and would have not needed to probe further. Rather I could have advised perseverance and continued fidelity to the full hour of prayer.

Listening to another as well as to oneself is listening to the Holy Spirit. Out of this we discern the will of God, and in this discernment we find our peace and joy. This is the whole point of spiritual direction—to know as accurately as possible God's will for us and to seek obediently to respond to that will in the day-to-day of our lives.

While this is the special task of the director, all of us are called to listen to the Holy Spirit. It is inherent in the call given to every Christian to love one another. For good listeners are good lovers, and they both demand perseverance and a lot of hard work.

Once I remember working with a directee in which this value of listening attentively may be further illustrated.

There was a quiet shyness about her, an air of simplicity and helplessness. When we first talked I sensed a woman steeped in the world of the Spirit, one who found worldly achievements, material gains, and the like foreign. The initial conversation was stilted, giving me not an impression of reserve, but a genuine inability on her part to express herself on spiritual things.

I asked her to tell me about her daily prayer. She began with brief statements, outlining more the mechanics of her prayer than the prayer itself. One hour a day she set aside for meditation, frequently during the week she attended Mass, and weekly she attended a prayer group. Slowly she warmed up to the subject, however, and proceeded to outline some of her prayer experiences.

They were profound. The Lord had steeped her in intimate experiences of his love for her, tangibly allowing her to experience—through moments of intense peace, a sense of abiding confidence in her worthwhileness in his eyes, a deep sense of being quite unworthy of this, and so on—a perception of who she was as a creature. She felt totally dependent on him for her daily life, and she was conscious of eternal salvation chiefly in the context of her day-to-day response to his love.

I was sensing by now a person very intimate with the Lord, but I suspended any judgment until I received more data. I asked her how long this prayer of love had lasted. It had been present only for a few months, though prior to that she had had momentary experiences that were similar. Listening to myself I was still not sure of her authenticity, so I decided to question with a little more bluntness.

"Have you experienced much pain in your life? Have you felt the effects of failure and sin?" They were routine questions, but they surfaced the reason for my feelings of disharmony.

She had been in religious life for many years and had gone through several traumatic experiences there. She had felt rejection and a real unacceptedness of her by her sister religious. She endured this for years out of a sense of obligation to her vows, but finally she had made the decision to leave. It was painful. She felt very much a failure, and in fact she had to see a psychiatrist for some months after she left in order to come to terms with her anger and resentment. Curiously enough, she turned to meditative prayer after her departure and found much security and consolation in it, whereas prayer in religious life had at best been a burdensome task that she did because she had to.

Her story revealed to me the ingredient I had felt missing before and gave me a sense of peace about her profound experiences of God's love for her. Listening to myself I trusted the harmony I now found there and encouraged her to continue her meditations on the Lord's love for her. In her story of failure and subsequent surrendering to the Lord out of that, the authentication of her present experiences of consolation in prayer was to be found. I merely urged her to enjoy them and to allow the Lord to continue doing what he willed with her heart. She agreed and left, at peace with my suggestion.

When she returned, I asked her to review what had ensued in her prayer. I had given her various passages on God's love from the Old Testament, not feeling the need to move her anywhere else, since she was seemingly deriving much consolation from his love.

Her prayers were moving and deeply touching. The Lord had used the Scripture passages as focal points for visiting her with his love and had gifted her with many tears of joy and peace. I felt harmony about it all and decided that it might be time to get her to question what she was about in this life. I did this by giving her a series of questions, not so much to answer, but to reflect on before the Lord, allowing the Scripture passages on his love that I had previously given her to be the focal point for her prayer. I asked her to group the questions into twos or threes or any way she chose, and then to meditate on the Scripture passage of her choice, with the questions forming a semi-conscious backdrop to her prayer.

I did this because I felt that the Lord was calling her to something beyond her present state—living alone in an apartment, teaching during the day—and felt that she could benefit from a grounding in her life's direction. Some of the questions ran as follows:

1. What is the purpose of my life at this time? Do I feel that this purpose is being realized? If so, why? If not, why not?
2. What do I feel guilty about most often? Why? How do I get rid of my guilt?
3. Looking back on my life, do I feel that I have gotten a "fair deal"? What does that mean to me?
4. What does it take for me to be true to myself? Is it important to me? Why?
5. What does it mean to me to be free? Do I feel that I am free? If so, why? If not, why not?
6. What is the one quality that I really like about myself? Why?
7. What are the things that I find have most meaning for me in life? Try to explain why.
8. Where is it most easy for me to find God?
9. Which person, or persons, of the Blessed Trinity do I find greatest ease praying to?
10. Do I feel God calling me in my heart (i.e., feelings) to any special place with him at this point in my life?

After I finished dictating the questions, I asked her to recall the initial feeling she had as she first heard the questions and to begin her prayer from that feeling. I explained that since each question took her unawares, the feeling reaction to it would most likely contain the truth and would be the answer to listen to. I told her to give me a call when she felt that her meditations had moved her in a definite direction, but that either way she was not to let the next appointment go for more than a month. I also urged her to make repetition meditations on all of the Scripture passages as well as the questions, pointing out the importance of relistening in her heart to the spirits within her, allowing the repetitions to authenticate or deny her first experience in any given prayer.

She agreed with my suggestions and direction, leaving with a sense of trust and some trepidation, not being sure what the questions would lead to. Neither did I, though I felt confident that the Spirit of truth would certainly make himself felt, given her openness and evident trust in God.

Three weeks passed before she called me. We set up an appointment for the next day, and I recall wondering where her prayer had led her. She had found the questions initially unresponsive. The feelings she had experienced when I first gave her the questions did not speak to her heart when she returned to them. In fact the Scripture passages had also lost their intensity, and for a while she thought that she was doing something wrong.

It was on the repetitions that the Lord started to make his presence evident. It was a quiet movement, much like the "gentle breeze" of Elijah. She began to feel a calmness in the questions and their answers. Most of them centered around a single response: "I am your God. I know what I am doing with you. Be not afraid." But when she sought practical implications of this refrain, the Lord remained silent, merely affirming for her, repeatedly, that he was enough and that there was nothing else that she needed.

I listened to two responses within me. One was of a slight disappointment—a sign that I was unconsciously expecting "signs and wonders" from her prayer. The other was a sense of peace, a conviction that the Lord had indeed spoken to her especially and that she was more at peace now than during her last visit—perhaps not peace as much as a greater conviction that her life had meaning, that it was going somewhere, and the "where" of the journey was toward him.

The intense love she had felt from him appeared to be taking on a new dimension. Previously it was a delightful, peace-filled experience that gave her a sense of being loved. Now, while all this remained true, it started appearing to her, not as a series of isolated delights, but as part of a process, and in a strange way it was also the end of the process. As I shared these reflections with her she nodded slowly and then blurted out that she almost felt the Lord calling her to share this life of hers with others. I wasn't sure what she meant, so I asked her to elaborate, but she wasn't sure either. Therefore I suggested that we listen to it in prayer and allow the Holy Spirit to enlighten her on its meaning by asking him, as a prelude to her daily meditations, to give her true wisdom to know his will. I suggested that we pray on "journey" passages appearing in the Old as well as the New Testaments, with particular emphasis on Jesus' journey to Jerusalem. She liked that, and wondered what she was being called to. "Whatever it is," I replied, "if we continue to be open to his Spirit, it has to be good."

She called me up a week later and asked for an appointment as soon as possible. Sensing that something had happened in her prayer that was significant—she had never pushed for an appointment before—I told her to come over.

When I saw her, her face was flushed, and there was an excited sparkle in her eyes. "I think the Lord wants me to be a contemplative," she said. "At least, I have been overcome with feelings of intense joy when I think about it." Suspending judgment again, I asked her when this thought first came to her mind. "In prayer," she replied, "out of nowhere, accompanied by waves of peace." I listened intently, feeling some disharmony within me, and yet uncertain as to its origin. She was evidently in consolation, seemingly peaceful and happy, yet something didn't click. I asked her to describe her prayer over the week in some detail.

She had prayed, faithful to her hour and to the readings suggested. She had set aside any direct meditating on where the Lord was leading her and was content to allow the passages to strike her as they willed, not attempting to force any issues. The movement toward the contemplative life began out of a meditation on Mary where, after Jesus was found among the doctors of the law, Mary "stored up all these things in her heart." To me her prayer sounded honest and open to the workings of the Spirit, but I wasn't sure, and either way I knew that this called for a process of discernment and not an instinctive response. She agreed, understandably a trifle disappointed at my apparent lack of enthusiasm, and we left it at that for the present. I suggested that she return to those passages that had touched her or repelled her the most over the past week and to continue asking the Holy Spirit for guidance, and we left it at that.

The next three or four meetings alternated between more contemplations on God's love, with few words and much peace, and meditations on Scripture about the life of our Lord. I had told her to avoid actively bringing up her thoughts about the contemplative life but to allow them to emerge if they so chose to do so in her prayer. It was a period of active waiting and of attentive listening. Gradually I found that we talked less about the contemplative life and more about freedom and her current delight in being so free to pray and to be alone with the Lord.

It emerged slowly, almost surreptitiously. She wanted to form her own community, to form a house of prayer where people with similar desires could come to find the Lord. They would be people intent on both finding the Lord in silence and sharing their home with others of similar longings. They would live in community but would retain their regular jobs, pooling their salaries for the upkeep of the place. It would not be a "religious community" in the technical sense of the word but would certainly contain parallels. They would take private vows of celibacy, but that was all.

Again I was cautious, though far less so than the previous time, for I sensed an authenticity in the peace this time that in some indecipherable way was absent on the previous occasion. I suggested that we take it to prayer and offer it up as a gift to the Spirit, praying for the grace of "indifference" in this, as just another earthly thing that in itself was not God.

She did, and the summation of it was neither the alternative nor its negation. It came to her out of her prayer: to take private vows of celibacy, continue living as she was, and allow her idea of a community of solitude and prayer to remain, but only as a future possibility and not as an immediate necessity.

I was at peace with this and urged her to continue challenging the various movements of the Spirit, not permitting an untested feeling to predominate and drive her actions, and always to stay close to the truth that apparently continued to work powerfully in her.

She took her vows, is leading a life of both action—through her teaching—and contemplation—through her solitary and prayer-oriented state of life—and remains content in allowing her dream of a house of contemplative prayer to wait for the future.

Listening to the various movements of the spirits and acting on them in the context of faith is a vital requirement for one engaged in spiritual direction. Often the movements are subtle, and a good director has to be most alert, aware that the Lord's will is being incarnated in the conversation with his retreatant, and that listening to one's directee with attention and devotion can be the only missing ingredient that can prevent, or at least obfuscate, that action of divine love. Directors need to always do their best to make sure this does not happen.

The Training of a Director

"Come to me, all you who labor and are overburdened, and I will give you rest" (Mt. 11:28). To enable this invitation of Jesus to become realized in people's hearts and minds, directors put their talents and training at the disposal of all those who want to respond to this invitation.

Elsewhere I have stated that two qualities are necessary for one seeking to direct others in the spiritual life. They are an ability to discern the various movements of the spirits in another, and a nurturing of that ability through training. I will now attempt to elaborate on what exactly I mean when I speak of the training of a spiritual director.

The training of a director begins with deciphering the longing in one's heart and mind to go out to others and bring to them the freedom, peace, and abundant life that the Spirit of Jesus brings. It is a vocation within our Christian vocation and calls us to respond to the invitation of Jesus to "love one another as I have loved you" (Jn. 15:12) in a particular way. It really begins when we first agree to become adult Christians, for are we not all called to "bring good news to the poor, to bind up hearts that are broken, to proclaim liberty to captives, freedom to those in prison" (Is. 61:1)? Yet some are better in one gift while others are more effective in another. Hence, while one may bind up a broken heart through wise teaching or writing, another may do so through spiritual direction. As St. Paul says, "there is a variety of gifts but always the same Spirit" (1 Cor. 12:4).

It may be worth repeating here that the gift of directing others is not the domain of priests and religious alone. A Christian who sincerely feels called to help others develop their spiritual lives—be that person a banker, a lawyer or a laborer—can very effectively become an instrument of God's healing love for others. Indeed the dearth of spiritual directors today and the rising number of Christians who are seeking direction ought to act as strong incentives to lay Christians, men and women, Catholics and Protestants, to ask themselves seriously whether they are willing and able to undertake this vocation within their baptismal commitment, for the good of many. This section is offered to all Christians who may wish to find out how to go about becoming a director.

Deciphering whether one possesses the gifts necessary for directing begins, it seems to me, at the feet of the Giver of all gifts, and this happens in prayer. If one finds a longing to pray, and if one responds to that longing by actually praying—and by prayer I mean the intimate listening of meditation and the like—one is taking the first step toward becoming a trained director. For a director is first of all a person who prays, and the first prerequisite for one who seeks to help others pray is to pray oneself.

From this flows the second prerequisite. The beginning pray-er begins to recognize the need for some guidance in prayer and seeks out a spiritual director. It seems to me that in these regular encounters with one's own director, much of the later astuteness that one may acquire is derived. This is not only a prerequisite, though. No person should direct another without having a spiritual director for oneself as well.

Presuming these two general prerequisites are fulfilled, then a potential director could think about making an eight-day directed retreat. This should be discerned with one's director, of course, and entered into only after both are in agreement that one is ready to make an eight-day retreat. By "ready" I do not mean prepared, as if one is preparing for an ordeal. It is quite ludicrous to look upon a directed retreat as an ordeal anyway, though some do. Rather, what is meant by "ready" is this: Is one truly wanting to enter deeper into the life of the Spirit, or is the motivation less pure in its intent? For example, a person who has served as a teacher in religious life may now be searching for a different "profession" and decide that spiritual direction is as good as any. This person may be then told that a directed retreat is a prerequisite to becoming a director, and so the person endures it, more like fulfilling a requirement in boot camp than feeling the yearning to enter personally into the life of the Spirit. This would hardly be the true spirit in which to fulfill this requirement.

Then—and this presumes several months of time, in fact preferably a year after the first directed retreat—the potential director may, again in partnership with a director, determine the time for making a full month's directed retreat.

During the interim a potential director ought to be engaged in studying various disciplines as a preparation to taking up this ministry. It seems to me, for example, that a spiritual director should have some knowledge of psychology. I think a good gauge of the amount of psychology you need can be summed up this way: Can you discern when a particular directee has a problem that goes beyond spiritual direction and is, in fact, outside the sphere of your own expertise? When you can determine that, you have the psychology you need to direct others.

Further, a future director should certainly know Sacred Scripture. A prime vehicle for God to work in our hearts is his own word. A director should know that word and be able to use it with some facility. And this knowledge must not be only book learning but the sort of knowledge that can occur only when one "relishes" the word in prayer. In conjunction with this, it could be of great benefit for a director to read and reflect on the lives of the saints, especially the great pray-ers who for ages have been signs of God's power working in his people.

The eucharistic liturgy is central in our Christian lives. During a time of intense prayer, as in a directed retreat, its centrality is heightened. Hence a director certainly needs to study liturgy and learn how to make the Eucharist the high point of a retreatant's day. This is of prime importance, for God often speaks with a powerful eloquence through his Son Jesus at the table of their love for us. There ought to be no room for sloppy liturgies at any time, but during a retreat particular regard for the Eucharist is essential. It is up to the well-trained director to make sure that this is respected; this is done through personal study of liturgy and an understanding of the richness of the sacrament through frequent participation in communal liturgies, para-liturgies, and the like.

Another discipline crucial to the future director is knowledge and understanding of the various signs of the spirits. This is outlined in *The Spiritual Exercises of St. Ignatius*, but the practical application contained in the discernment of these spirits is to be derived only through practice. Since they are "exercises" the words of Ignatius are like a rule book for lifting weights. Seeing them in practice is the only bona fide way of understanding their workings. But can this be done? I think it begins in workshops for spiritual directors where role playing is a fundamental tool of learning. Then comes the internship where one directs under a "master director" who offers criticisms and suggestions as the direction progresses. In this dynamic between intern and master one soon comes to realize that all the theory, as valuable and as important as it is, often is far from the reality of the situation. "One learns by doing, just like a good teacher," a director once told me. I believe he was quite right.

A part of what one "learns by doing" is working with teams of directors. I have mentioned at various places the importance of teams when giving directed retreats. But there is a dynamic to be learned in working with teams, and the sooner it is learned the easier the task becomes. And the task is to enable the Spirit to touch another with love and peace. A team is a group of two or more directors and a staff that caters to the physical needs of everyone on the retreat. The size of both depends, of course, on the number of retreatants involved. Ideally they should come together at least twenty-four hours before the start of the retreat to get to know one another if they are strangers, or reacquaint themselves with each other if they are not. This day should be spent in prayer and in recreation. The team is going to be working quite closely with one another for the next several days; playing together is an excellent way of making the days to come be grace-filled and not tension filled. It is the task of the team leader to initiate this, as it would be that leader's duty to call the first of the team meetings during that day. This meeting needs to be a clarifier. Directors, being human, are usually in several different psychic and spiritual places. In this meeting they must be called upon to express what their hopes and expectations are for the retreat, what prayer form they are comfortable with when it comes to liturgy, and whether their understanding of retreat recollection includes or excludes informal get-togethers with the team daily. I think many retreat teams could avoid unnecessary tensions if these matters were clarified and openly discussed from the very outset.

A crucial issue that needs to be clarified in this meeting is the understanding of confidentiality during the retreat. It seems to me that it must be made evident that spiritual direction is not the sacrament of reconciliation. It is a careful tending of a soul who trusts that a director will be a true enabler of God's Spirit during a precious time in that person's life. Directors are called to make use of all the graces of the Spirit available, and one of the graces at a director's disposal is the presence of other directors. The analogy could be legitimately drawn between the confidentiality preserved by the medical profession and that of a team of spiritual directors. Frequently a doctor consults a colleague or a team of colleagues when uncertain of a diagnosis or treatment. Doctors maintain high ethical standards and preserve a strict confidentiality. The same can be legitimately expected from spiritual directors. A director, if uncertain of what spirits are at work in the retreatant, should, after seeking the retreatant's permission and promising to preserve his or her anonymity, be able to consult with the team or with one member on the team for advice and suggestions. In this way the spirits that seek to confuse can be, with a greater facility, subverted.

Once I remember experiencing considerable frustration over what I thought was a retreatant's refusal to cooperate with the Spirit. I felt that he was stubborn, not truly open to my suggestions and actually not very committed to making the retreat. I found that I was allowing my frustrations to turn into anger. Externally I preserved an air of graciousness, but within my negative feelings were getting the better of me.

At the team meeting that day I talked to my fellow directors about my feelings. They listened attentively to my complaint and empathized with me. But then one of them said, "I feel that the problem is not really with your retreatant but with you. From what you are telling me I feel that you are taking entirely too much responsibility for your retreatant's progress." I found resentment building up inside me. I listened to him, but inwardly I was telling myself, "Even you, my fellow director, do not understand what I am going through!" But then another director broke in and said, "I think Jim is right. I too feel discomfort about your over-involvement with your retreatant." I listened, and then, after a pause, I asked, "What should I do?" He replied, "I think you need to just lay back and not try to force things. Also, set aside any expectations that you may have of your retreatant. Just turn him over to God's grace and try to be his companion in prayer, not his leader." The other director on the team agreed. He said, "I think that's sound advice. It seems that what is happening here is a symptom of the evil spirit trying to frustrate you to such an extent that you are being rendered ineffectual." I continued to listen and felt slightly humiliated and guilty. In my efforts to help the retreatant I was interfering with God and his plans. I thanked my co-directors and said that I would follow their advice. After the meeting I prayed, and as I further interiorized what they were saying I felt a peace well up from within.

The next day I saw my retreatant again. He had had another frustrating day and felt that he was getting nowhere. Following my co-directors' advice, I suppressed the desire to suggest another "spiritual tactic" to him and instead merely said: "Don't worry about it." He looked at me uncertainly. I went on to tell him that I felt we were both trying too hard. "Why don't we just relax today?" I said. "Maybe you can just go for a long walk through the woods, enjoy the trees and the flowers, and not feel any pressure to meditate on Sacred Scripture. The Lord will come in his way, not ours." I asked him how he felt about that. "Great," he said. "I need the break. I feel very tense."

That day he rested—and that day God visited him. He related to me how even as he was strolling among the trees he started feeling a sense of peace begin to change his frustration. He simply allowed it to do so and continued to enjoy nature. He resisted the temptation to "pray" and felt a joy emanate from inside him. It developed as the day wore on, and not long afterward he experienced God's love for him in a calm, non-spectacular way through a gentle tranquility that he felt as a tangible sign of God's caring love. The rest of his retreat continued in this vein and I continued to "lay back," letting the Spirit direct his son in his ways.

Working with a team of directors who astutely perceived where I was going wrong enabled the spirits of frustration and anger to be replaced by the Holy Spirit, yielding a harvest of joy and peace and love to my retreatant as well as for myself.

Sometimes, however, working on a team can be difficult. It would be unrealistic to expect all teams to jell and all directors to be of a like spiritual vein. Indeed if that were the case some potential graces could become obscured by a team who may hold a single method of directing as paramount over another. Directors as well as directees are of various hues and shades, and it is most important that one recognize this when joining a team of people who are relative strangers. There are differences of opinion that frequently prevail, and a well trained director ought to be one sufficiently open to the Spirit to comfortably accept these differences by choosing to respect one's co-director even though disagreeing with a particular director's approach. Perhaps the commonest example of this is seen between the directive and non-directive approaches to spiritual direction. The former type believes in a firm guidance of the directee; the latter believes in a supportive listening that allows the directee to arrive at a given insight on one's own. Both have validity and both can enable the Spirit to emerge. But I think if a given director on a team asserts that only one of these forms works, a difficult and possibly tension-filled situation among the team can result. It is important that directors respect one another and trust that the Spirit can work effectively through whatever method the director finds most comfortable.

This mutual respect, however, ought not to preclude an honest sharing of opinion among directors. Often it could be precisely this interchange that can make a director see that while in the main a particular form of direction is effective, one ought to be open to seeing that in a given situation another less personally appealing form could be more effective. A trained director is hence one capable of listening not just to the movements within the directee but also to those gentle reminders offered by one's team that often can call one to an openness in directing that could benefit oneself as well as the directee.

Team meetings ought to be a regular part of a day's schedule during a directed retreat. The format may vary, depending on the majority opinion of the team. However, it seems to me that a meeting ought to include time for prayer, a liturgy planning session, and a time when directors who may need to discuss a particular difficulty can do so. Once I was on a team that added to this by asking each director to give a presentation on what one considered one's particular specialty in spiritual direction. Consequently each day one of us presented a reflection on such topics as discerning the spirits, the Ira Progoff intensive journal method, the varieties of prayer and the like. I found the presentations very interesting and learned much about matters that I had only a slight knowledge of before. But I remember feeling some pressure inside me as well, for I felt that as valuable as the talks were, the forum of the team meeting was not necessarily the best one for them. I think this was because I found that at times the presentation seemed to be taking precedence over the matter at hand which was the retreat and its progress. However, I do think that such matters could be worked into team meetings with efficacy so long as the pressures of time and exhaustion are adequately taken into account by the team members. Certainly it provided us with a greater appreciation of one another as directors and as people who possessed an expertise on matters that taken together made us better directors. And this may have very well been partially responsible for the mutual trust that developed among us as that retreat progressed. However, I think that sensitivity to one another ought to be the governing force behind the format of the team meeting.

But often there is no team. Often one is involved in direction and has no recourse to a fellow director. At times like this it is very important that one have within easy access a colleague who can be reached in case any difficulty arises. This becomes especially true when one is giving ongoing spiritual direction.

Ongoing spiritual direction differs from direction within the context of a retreat in that it takes place in the context of a person's day-to-day life. During a retreat the experience of God is heightened, and the distractions are reduced to a minimum through such well-known essentials as retreat silence; in ongoing direction the Spirit is to be found in the events of a person's daily life, heightened in the prayer period. In a retreat one deals with the movements of the spirits occurring exclusively in a person's prayer, while in ongoing direction one has to incorporate and take heed of the influence of events in a person's life as well as the person's prayer. This is not to say that the events of a person's life are excluded during a retreat. That would be ridiculous. Rather, in retreat direction the emphasis is primarily on the movements of the spirits in prayer, influenced only in a participatory way by the events of a person's life. In ongoing direction the life events of a person take on far more significance. It is the task of the director to learn, primarily through experience, to differentiate between these two dynamics of direction, and hence to become flexible in utilizing the one or the other as the need arises.

A spiritual director's training never ends. It must be ongoing, even as spiritual direction occurs both in the heightened spiritual climate of a retreat and on a day-to-day basis. A director needs to allow the training of his apprenticeship to become the training of the master. In other words, spiritual directors always need to be persons of prayer, always need other spiritual directors to help ongoing discernment for themselves, and hence need to be always open to the Spirit's "gentle breeze" in their own lives.

A Competent Incompetent

I started my work in spiritual direction some years prior to ordination, and often during those times priests would ask me how I did it. I was compelled to recognize through these questions that in their minds there was an association between priesthood and spiritual direction that I had not been made aware of. Also, the questions challenged me to ask myself how I *did* do it. What was there within me that enabled me to direct other people in spiritual matters? The questioning also forced me to listen to the discomfort I felt in the presumption behind the questions. Did the priesthood, in some sort of magical way, confer talent upon people which made it possible for them to direct others?

The competence of the spiritual director is linked to holy orders in that both priests and spiritual directors are supposed to help people pray. But all priests are not spiritual directors, even as all spiritual directors are not priests. The religious, the lay person, and the priest who seek to aid another in the spiritual life must first explore their competence in the work, seek help and guidance in it and always allow themselves to be awed at the potential gift God is offering them in their own spiritual lives. For to direct others benefits one's own spiritual life immeasurably, and in all probability directors benefit more from their directees than vice versa.

Qualified directors are those who are aware of their own incompetence to direct another in the awesome and sacred work of leading another to God. At the same time directors know that they do possess competence, derived from prayer and training, that has fostered the God-given talent of discernment. The director is in many ways, a paradox, both capable and incapable, a competent incompetent—competent in having the expertise, but quite incompetent in effecting the healing or the growth that people seek in spirituality. This incompetence, perhaps, is what sets the spiritual director apart from other secular professions. To be effective as a spiritual director one is in partnership, and one can never be effective if this partnership is not actively and constantly fostered.

This partnership is with God, who is the director of his people, as well as with the directee. Competent directors recognize their incompetence without the Spirit, and accordingly they strain to hear this Spirit in the many ways he is made audible.

Emphasizing this incompetence may appear unnecessary. It is something we all know about and presume. Of course God is the real director, and obviously without him we could do nothing. Unfortunately, it is an emphasis that needs to be made, for it is a presumption that on occasion is not made. No amount of professional training, as essential as it is, can qualify a person to direct another if the Holy Spirit is not recognized as the primary director. It is a feeling one needs to have in one's heart as well as in one's mind, and the more expert one becomes, the more this basic truth is to be remembered and listened to with greater intent.

Let me relate an instance of this from my own experience. I was dealing once with a person who had murdered his closest friend of many years. Now he was filled with remorse and was in a state of profound depression. He came to me for some understanding and for God's forgiveness. He had excoriated himself many a time, in prayer and out of prayer, but the guilt and the fear of God's retribution had not abated.

When he had finished I talked slowly, uncertain of how to proceed. I assured him that God's forgiveness was indeed his, that God's love is for all people and no one is turned away no matter what the gravity of the sin. I pointed out that the proof of this was the fact that he was sitting there telling me about it and begging God's forgiveness. "His love," I went on, "is steeped in mystery, and the mystery of his love is evident right now in you, in this room, as you ask to be forgiven." I wasn't sure what else to say, so I kept on in this vein for a while. Gradually I felt some semblance of peace in him. I kept repeating to him that God had forgiven him, that his remorse was caused by God's grace in him, and that it was quite clear to me that he was deeply sorry for what he had done. So far I was operating out of my training, but while he was beginning to calm down, nothing in my expertise had prepared me for what I did next.

I suggested that he write a letter. He said he had done that—to his wife. (His wife had left him after his arrest.) I replied, "No, not to your wife—to your neighbor, your brother whom you killed." He looked at me incredulously and then smiled weakly in understanding. I told him to tell his murdered friend how sorry he was for killing him and beg his forgiveness. He left me, looking forward to it.

The next day he came in and handed me a piece of paper: the letter. He had struggled all night and finally had it as he wanted it. It was a powerful letter, simple but profound. He told me that he cried all the way through the writing of it. Then, feeling much better, he asked me, "Now what?" I said, "Let's give it to him." Again he looked incredulous. In response I told him to give it to me before Mass and I would offer it up at the Eucharist, to God, who would most certainly deliver it to his friend.

He liked the idea. At the Eucharist he was subdued but at times visibly moved. Afterward he told me that during the liturgy he felt his friend's forgiveness, and in that process he felt God forgiving him as well. He believed that he could face the trial and the jail sentence to come. He was at peace with himself. Here was the Holy Spirit at work. Looking back on that suggestion I recall a feeling of rightness about it prior to suggesting it to him. It came peacefully and with some accompanying doubt as to its appropriateness.

But then, trusting in the Spirit working in the moment, I proposed it. The ensuing results caused a peace and a new trust in God for him that my competence alone could never have effected.

A spiritual director is aware that a loving Father-Son-Spirit never fails to reach out and touch the wounded son or daughter in our midst. It is the duty of the spiritual director to be as enabling as possible in this process of love so that the love of God may be realized in this world. Hence the good director needs to be comfortable with the non-directive as well as the more emphatic ways of a firmer guidance. One should not be preoccupied with technique or form. Rather one ought to feel sufficiently free to use whatever method appears most suitable for the good of the directee.

It is the opinion of some that spiritual directors work with people who are, by and large, living in a somewhat rarefied atmosphere distanced from the "real world" with all its brutality and hatred. While to an extent there is some truth to this, it would be quite incorrect to presume that spiritual direction is given only to the devout and the daily Mass-goer.

Sometimes a director does come face-to-face with one not very steeped in the spiritual life, in fact living in a world that is quite apart from it. At times like this a director is compelled to rely even more heavily than usual on his faith. That gives him the firm assurance that the incompetence he may feel in such an encounter is rendered into a competence that comes from the Spirit working in and through him. Let me tell you of such an experience I once had that found me "treading foreign soil" and paradoxically feeling secure. I hope it will illustrate this paradox of a competent incompetent a little better.

He was an undercover police officer who was daily confronted with the dregs of society. He knew all of the underworld bigwigs and had dedicated his life to their downfall. Many a time he had witnessed the consequences of their actions. Anger was something he lived with daily.

When he came in to see me he was confused about the spiritual side of his life and needed guidance in it. He was a regular church-goer who prayed daily for guidance from God and for the wisdom to know right from wrong. In his work he was constantly confronted by a tension between the Christian message of love and forgiveness that he firmly believed in, and the world of deceit and lies that he daily worked with.

I asked him to elaborate on his confusion. He said, "Often I have to ferret out the truth from suspects in a way that I know is not right. Especially when I'm working on a big case, the outcome of which I know will affect dozens of lives, I feel I have to make promises and threats that I know are lies." I asked him to get specific, pointing out that it was possible that "the lies" he was referring to might not be as bad as he judged them to be. Actually I felt uncertain within myself as to what to tell him; I was simply looking for more data before we could go on. On the one hand, I told myself, here is a man who for years has been to the sacraments, made retreats throughout his adult life, and was evidently intent on being as a good a Christian as possible. On the other he was working in a world quite strange to me, and one in which the powers of evil continuously triumphed.

He went on: "You see, when I witness a murder or a severe beating ordered by a person that I know, a bigwig who is so powerful that the highest officials in the state wouldn't dare touch him, I get very angry. I am willing to do anything to try to capture him and put him away for life. This is made even worse because the victims are usually small-time hoods who just learned too much and had to be eliminated. Many times I know they don't even have the knowledge they are suspected of having, but if they are suspected it is enough to have them killed. It is terrible, just terrible! So, when I get on the case, I feel a strong drive, deep inside me, to catch the murderer, and I am willing to do anything to effect that capture."

While he was talking the disciplined control on his expression that he had carried with him into my office was beginning to release a bit. I started noting genuine signs of emotion on his face. I felt a little relieved because I knew that if he could feel in the retelling then he wasn't the hardened cop that he initially made himself out to be. I asked him to go on.

"Well," he said, "I have many snitches on the streets. They are usually first and second offenders out for a few months, or maybe even a year. They always come back," he said with a wry smile. "Anyway, I guarantee them protection from us if they feed me enough information. Well, the thing of it is, I make those guarantees with little basis in fact. I mean, I don't have the power it takes to keep them from the slammer when it comes right down to it. What I do is use them to get the information I want on the bigger fish, but I can only do my best to keep them out of the slammer if they get caught."

Fascinated by his story I asked, "What has been your success rate in this?"

"Well, through God's grace I haven't done too badly so far, but the point is that I lie to them when I promise them immunity, and I don't like it at all."

"How many times have you succeeded in keeping them out?" I asked.

He paused briefly, and then, almost with a triumphant grin, he told me: "Nine times out of ten."

"That's not a bad batting average, is it?" I said, smiling. He nodded his head in agreement. "So perhaps," I went on, "you are not lying to them as much as you think you are. Let me ask you this. When you promise them that you will protect them, do you mean it?"

"Of course," he replied. "Definitely, and I do my best every time to take care of them."

"Good," I said. "Then it appears you haven't been intending to lie to them." He smiled. I went on: "You see, if your motivation when you promised them protection was truthful—and it seems to me that it was—you're doing all right before God."

He seemed relieved, and sat silently for several moments, letting that sink in. I waited. Then he said, "Thank you. That helps a lot. Now, I have another problem."

"Go on," I said, "I'm listening."

"Well," he started, "in my work I am in a tough world. It's kill or be killed. Often I have to fight someone, and often I beat him up more than I should. In the heat of the moment, I guess I lose my head. Also, since I do a lot of my work at night, I get into situations that are very tense, and I go for my gun many a time when there is no need for it."

"Do you fire it?" I asked.

"Well, sometimes, but I guess my training prevents me from firing until I'm sure."

"All right," I said, "let's go back to the first thing you said—that you sometimes beat a person up more than you should. Now, I don't begin to say that I understand the world you work in, so all my reflections are coming from my world and my understanding of your problem."

"That's what I want," he said. "I'm too close to it to be able to come up with a solution."

"Fine," I went on. "Now let's get our facts straight first. How often do you have to rough somebody up?"

"Oh, two or three times a month," he said.

"And, of these times do you first try to reason with them?"

"Oh, yes," he said, "every time. It's always a last resort, and even with my training in self-defense I'm always a little scared to get into a fight. You see, I don't look like a cop since I work undercover, and often when I show my badge, that can provoke them even more rather than subdue them. Also, it's hard to call for help, especially the places I end up in." I nodded. "But," he went on, "the trouble is, when I get into it I want to beat the man's brains out. That's what gets to me."

"I see," I said, uncertain as to how to proceed. "Well, do you actually do it?" I asked, "I mean, do you beat his brains out?"

"Sometimes," he said. "I've put a few of them in the hospital, and afterward I feel terrible."

"Have you been put in the hospital?" I asked.

"Oh, yes," he replied, "two or three times."

"So it works both ways," I said.

He nodded.

I was aware that I was treading alien ground, but I whispered a silent prayer for guidance. I sensed a keen attentiveness in me and began to feel the glimmer of a possible lead coming to me. Trusting in the Spirit guiding me, I went on. "Let's sit back and look at the total picture," I said. "Here you are in a tense, dangerous situation and your life is threatened—every day, in fact. You are up against odds you don't know anything about. You overreact. Right?"

He nodded.

"Now," I said, "why are you in that situation in the first place?"

"It's my job," he said.

"But why are you in this job?"

"To make the streets safe—to protect our people," he replied. "I really want to do that."

"So your motivation comes out of a desire to take care of your fellow men, to love them. And you put your life on the line daily for that?"

"Yes, I guess so," he replied.

I pressed my point. "You don't go out there to beat someone up, do you?"

"No," he said, "not at all. I hate doing it, and I do it only when I have to."

Again I paused and asked myself, "What would Jesus do in a similar situation?" When he was with the Pharisees or the scribes he certainly stood up to them, but he did so with constraint, coupled with a definite firmness. I shared my thoughts with him, reminding him of the way Jesus handled similar situations. I pointed out that overreaction in such situations was normal, and I suggested that he start meditating on specific passages in Scripture where Jesus was faced with threats and attacks. I was feeling an increasing confidence within me by now, and so I followed that feeling. I told him to concentrate on Jesus' ways, to keep always in mind the motivation that took him out to the streets in the first place, and to continue to be honest with himself and his conscience. "The Lord alone can give you the constraint you need," I went on. "Meanwhile don't be too hard on yourself. God knows the whole picture, and he is a just judge. This is something we cannot solve right now, but what we need to do is initiate a process of sensitization, making you aware of what happens to you at that particular moment in the fight when you lose control and continue to beat your assailant excessively. I suggest that you ask Jesus to be with you when you know a fight is brewing and trust that he will watch over you during it. I know this is not much, but it's all that's coming to me right now."

He smiled. "I think that will do," he said. "Maybe this is what I'm looking for. I'll try it. I'll start meditating daily, if you'll show me how, and ask God to be with me at those times."

That evening I taught him the rudiments of meditation, suggested some Scripture passages, and urged him to stick to about twenty minutes of prayer a day for the first month, increasing it to a half hour or so from then on.

"Sound O.K.?" I asked.

"Yes," he replied. "I feel I now have something definite to work with. I feel I have a sort of spiritual weapon now!" He grinned and said, "You know, I feel relieved, as though I have a program to follow that will keep me safe with God."

"I'm glad," I said. "Feel free to return for another chat if you feel the need."

"Thanks," he said and left.

I recall feeling a sense of uncertainty as I watched him leave. I also felt a little foolish, aware that the world he was living in was quite foreign to me and that my suggestions probably seemed somewhat irrelevant to the grim and "down to earth" experiences of his daily life. Yet I consoled myself that he left my office somewhat hopeful and appeared satisfied with our chat. After all, he had returned in the evening to learn how to meditate. Maybe that was a sign that that was the thing to do. I wasn't sure. I knew that the guarantee I was looking for—that I had responded to his needs with competence—would not be forthcoming. I had to trust in the competence of the Lord, and I prayed that I would do so in faith.

Looking back on that conference, what I remember is a process of faith evolving in me, from an initial state of experiencing my own incompetence to help him, to a slowly evolving realization that I needed to let go of that fear so that the Lord could help him through me. As I questioned him I felt this happening. As I prayed silently for help I knew that the Lord was hearing me by the gradual sense I had of knowing the way to proceed with my questioning and by the eventual suggestions I made to help him in his need.

The potential spiritual director is called to remember always that the competent Spirit of God is ever ready to help him in his incompetence. The Spirit yearns to bring guidance and healing to all who seek it with a sincere heart and eagerly assists the director who is uncertain of how to proceed in a given situation, thus bringing the healing and direction the directee is seeking with unfailing fidelity.

Another instance of this paradox can perhaps even better illustrate what I am talking about here. It was an encounter that called out of me a change of heart and that enabled the Spirit to touch the retreatant with love, making out of my initial weakness and fear a transforming feeling of strength. That, in turn, led to a moment of grace for a retreatant.

She was a university dean as well as chairperson of several civic committees in her city, very involved in the politics of her school. Tall, with a domineering attitude, she walked into my office exuding an air of superiority and boredom. I had immediate feelings of being intimidated and inferior to her. Noting them, I told myself sternly that the Lord was the true director of the retreat, that I was only his instrument, and that my task was to be open to his Spirit and operate out of that openness. Besides, I told myself, her competence is not in this realm; I must trust myself and my own competence in directing her.

Before I had a chance to say much beyond our initial greeting she interrupted me, wanting to make a few things clear to me before we got any further. When she did, I felt resentment and anger building up inside me. I felt treated very much like a schoolboy who had not done his homework.

She informed me of her many obligations, both to the university community she worked in and to the town at large. "Consequently," she went, "I have several commitments that I cannot get out of during this week, and I'm afraid that I will have to leave the retreat a few times to meet them."

"How many?" I asked.

She proceeded to tell me. It turned out that just about every day of the retreat there was something she had to do, most of which entailed a long drive to and from the retreat house. There were also two cocktail parties and one dinner engagement that she had to make.

Surprisingly as she started enumerating her commitments I started feeling calmer and calmer, until I truly felt in charge of things. Ironically, since I was only listening and saying hardly anything, I got the impression that *she* was becoming more confident, with a tinge of sarcasm in her voice. She gave me the distinct indication that she knew she was in charge, so I had better watch out.

I recall clearly the change taking place in me as she was speaking. It was one of the more evident instances in my experiences of the Spirit taking my incompetence and putting in its place, deep within my heart, a sense of strength and security. I felt an increasing peace and a simultaneous feeling of courage. A sense of boldness was also beginning to be present and a desire to speak out, from my very soul, the truth that was being perceived there.

By the time she had finished talking I was thinking clearly and had no doubts as to my line of action. I started by asking her why she had come to this retreat, with those other commitments pending. She said it was because she had to make an annual retreat. She was a religious—and this was the only time she had during which she was relatively free to make one.

I nodded. Then, after a few moments of silence, I spoke, slowly and distinctly, with a sense of courageous peace that came from my depths: "You have stated your conditions for this retreat. Now, I will state mine," I began. "First, if you are really serious about putting God as center in your life I require that you cancel all your commitments for this week. This is to be done by one phone call, and it is to be done today. Second, I ask that you make a decision in your heart to surrender as best you can at this point to the process of this retreat and to the requirements inherent in it. That is: prayer, silence, and openness to your director. Third," I continued, "you need to recognize what your motives are in making this retreat—fulfilling an obligation. This is possibly quite the worst reason to come to this place. These are my conditions. If you want to stay on this retreat they are to be met. If not, I will be happy to refund your money to you, and you may leave. I will see you at two this afternoon to hear your decision. Now, this conference is over. You are free to leave."

She left, but she left very different from the way she walked in. Her face registered shock, and as she walked out of the room in silence she appeared slightly shaky, which was probably nothing in comparison to what I was feeling. But I was at peace with what I had done, and I knew that all I could do now was pray that God's will would win out in her. It was, for me, a clear sign of the Spirit taking my initial fear and ensuing incompetence and transforming it into his own competence.

The few hours before her afternoon appointment were difficult ones for me. I felt fear and uncertainty again. I worried that I had done the wrong thing, even though on a deeper level I knew I hadn't. I felt depression creeping in as I thought back on the conference; feelings of inferiority and inadequacy soon followed. I identified them, praying that the Lord would take them away from me. They persisted, but I was at peace as well. I recall glancing nervously at the parking lot a few times to see whether her car was still there. It was.

When the hour arrived I was calm, but I also felt my heart racing. When she knocked on the door, promptly at two, I said: "Come in." She did, looking quite subdued, almost crushed. The contrast to her morning entrance was as opposite as black is to white. Without inviting her to sit down I asked her, "Well, what have you decided?"

"I'll meet your conditions," she said. "I've already made my phone call and my commitments have been cancelled."

"Good," I responded. "Please sit down." She did.

Within me I sighed deeply and felt a great sense of relief. The Spirit had worked again with his people and had rendered them amenable to the loving overtures with which he longs to shower us—and this through a fear-filled weak person whom he transformed into a strong vehicle for his love. The rest of her retreat turned out to center on surrendering to God's will in her life, and on her religious perspective that had gradually placed God very much on the sidelines. It was a moving retreat, and it ended on a note of docility to the Spirit and a firm decision to pray daily so that she would not again close her lifeline to the Father.

Conclusion

In this chapter I have tried to describe some of the legitimate expectations one may have of a spiritual director, and hence what any potential director ought to expect if one is thinking about engaging in this most valuable work. These expectations are not comprehensive by any means, but hopefully they afford some help to all of us who need spiritual guides at some time or another in our lives. Accordingly, I have offered some major expectations of spiritual directors: that they be people of prayer, steeped in regular contact with God through a humble listening to him in their hearts and minds, that they be aware of their own vulnerability and so seek initial as well as ongoing training to develop the gift of discernment God has given them, that they know how important it is to listen attentively to the other, and, even though they are aware of their incompetence, that they be quite confident in God's competence to enable great changes to take place through them.

And changes are always for the better—for a happier life, a life more abundant than any of us dare dream possible, filled with good things given, through the power of him who loves us. It is my wish that many Christians, recognizing their own potential to direct others, will choose to realize this potential by seeking to meet these expectations and so become the directors of the future. "The harvest is rich, the laborers are few. . . ." (Lk. 10:2).

The invitation is for life abundant. It is given by God to all who believe in him. In this book I have tried to answer three questions designed around this exciting invitation. All that we dream about accomplishing, all our fondest hopes and most private longings can be realized if we but believe. In fact all that God longs for is our complete happiness. He said so through St. Paul: "I want you to be happy, always happy in the Lord; I repeat, what I want is your happiness" (Phil. 4:4).

Consequently the answer to my first question certainly was an all-encompassing one. Who needs spiritual direction? All of us do, in the sense that all of us need help to become the complete and whole human being that our inheritance in Christ Jesus calls us to receive. For it is in Jesus that the fulfillment of our deepest and most authentic longings are realized, and it is only because of him that we can walk through our lives with hope as our constant companion. But trying to lead lives of love—and is not the culmination of being fully human found in this?—brings with it struggle and sorrow. Yet we need to be reminded as the saying goes that "the greatest sorrow is not to love." In spiritual direction we receive these reminders and supports as we continue on our pilgrim way.

As one more support, I have offered the answer to my next question: What happens through spiritual direction? Here I tried to become specific in giving concrete instances of the Spirit at work. The examples are signs that the abundant life is ours if we want it and are willing to work for it. Many are the struggles inherent in fully responding to the invitation, for the forces of sin are all around us and seek constantly to subvert the gifts of the Holy Spirit that are given to us.

Finally I tried to outline some of the qualifications and characteristics one needs to look for in a spiritual director, remembering that all people intent on the spiritual life are potential directors. This chapter tried to describe how this potential could be evoked.

In describing the various movements of the Spirit I have compartmentalized, somewhat artificially, the gifts of the Holy Spirit. I did this to enhance appreciation of each of the gifts, though, of course, the Spirit's gifts cannot be divided. When we receive one, we receive more than one, and who can delineate where the one begins and the other ends? The Spirit allows his gifts to blend one into another even as each is distinct in itself.

The point of it all is life, and life more abundantly. For us who dare to dream of visions beyond, of worlds unknown and far removed from our day to day, the spirit world beckons and invites us into the life of God himself, to journey inward where God and his people can sit down at table in a timeless union of ever spending, never spent, love. The invitation is always extended, the journey is always just about to begin, for someone, somewhere.

The Spirit blows where he wills and does not know about restrictions when he chooses to love. His extravagance refuses to be limited to a certain number of gifts; they are limitless. "If all were written down, the world itself, I suppose, would not hold all the books that would have to be written" (Jn. 21:25).

Because of this I sense an incompleteness at the end of this writing, but also an exuberance that the Spirit promises so much more to come. He is with his people, eager for them to come to him, longing to shower them with good things, and hoping that daily more and more will come to delight in him and receive, however obscurely, the knowledge of his vision for each of us, a life of true peace, of potentials fully realized, of love complete in a perpetual blossoming.

"The Spirit and the Bride say, 'Come.' Let everyone who listens answer, 'Come.' Then let all who are thirsty come: all who want it may have the water of life, and have it free. . . . The one who guarantees these revelations repeats his promise: I shall indeed be with you soon. Amen. Come, Lord Jesus" (Rev. 22:17-20).